CORE JOY

CORE JOY

Cultivating Sustainable Deep Happiness

MIKE AUBÉ

Published and distributed worldwide by: Mike Aubé Spiritual Coaching,
Wolfville, NS, Canada. http://mikeaube.com

Editing, cover and interior design by David W. Edelstein
Author photo by Kimberley Bennett

Paperback ISBN: 978-1-7388468-0-1
E-book ISBN: 978-1-7388468-1-8
Audiobook ISBN: 978-1-7388468-2-5

CORE JOY

contents

God, Drugs and Rock & Roll

It was during the summer of my 25th year that I snapped.

I snapped and was plunged into a decade-long lost period, a time of confusion, frustration, depression and a desperate search for meaning. I snapped and was forced to question everything I had ever believed or had been told about reality. I snapped and lost my identity. I snapped and ceased to know joy.

Hardly anyone knew this about me, even though there were clues. From the outside, I'm sure I appeared the same old happy-go-lucky guy I always was. I had a wonderful girlfriend who became my wife two years later, I had great friends, I had a supportive family and I was working on a Master's degree in Kinesiology at the University of New Brunswick. I was on the right path to live a productive, successful and joyful life.

But make no mistake. On the inside, I had snapped. It

would be many years before I would recover. And it would be many years after *that* before I could say that I was living a life of joy. To understand why all this happened, we have to rewind a bit.

I was born to two school teachers on the outskirts of a tiny rural village of 700 people on the east coast of Canada. The closest kids my age lived over a mile away and 'town' was even further. I had two younger brothers and we were very tight, but I also spent a lot of time alone. Even well into my teens, my social life was limited to lunch and recess at school, and the sports teams that I played on (which were often coached by my dad because, you know, small town).

When you are a socially limited teachers' kid in a teeny town, let's just say a lot of your education comes from institutions – school, sports, television...and church. My family's history was generations upon generations of Roman Catholics, and we were no exception. If we were going to have to miss Mass on Sunday morning because of a basketball game, you bet your ass we were in church Saturday evening.

Strange as it may seem to some people, including my middle-aged agnostic mystic self, there was much about the church that I liked. Sure, it was boring at times, but the Catholic Church is kind of sexy. With its colourful robes, golden chalices and crosses, flickering candles and pungent incense, the pomp and pageantry can put you into a hypnotic state. I remember times just staring at a candle on the altar and letting my field of vision grey out, feeling as if my body were floating while the priest's words washed over me. There were times of psychedelic-like bliss. And the fantastic stories of Jesus walking on water, healing the sick and turn-ing water into wine were, let's face it, wildly entertaining and thought-provoking. So, religion was very influential on my early thinking, as was school.

I was good at school. I had to be. Not only were both my parents teachers at my elementary school, but my dad was the principal. Of course, everyone...everyone...expected me to be 'smart'. Much like with the church, even though school could be dull, I actually enjoyed learning. I was a curious kid, particularly when it came to science. I remember being enthralled with the simple experiments we did with magnet-ism and electricity, and trying to imagine what it would be like to be Einstein or Newton or Galileo, having these eureka moments and developing theories to explain the mysteries of the world around us.

All of this is to say that the institutions of Catholicism and public education (the science bits in particular) were the major forces that shaped my beliefs growing up. I should say at this point that I saw no conflict between science and religion. I felt that they were both attempts to explain a reality that was larger than either of them. Science was more logical and literal, while religion was magical and metaphorical. I could accept them both without it causing much of a rift in my mind.

Looking back, however, I can see that this was the seed of what caused me to snap many years later. The sun, water and soil that were poured on that seed, allowing it to sprout, grow and ultimately shade out my joy, were Art, the Internet and drugs.

As I have said, I spent a lot of time alone in my youth. During this alone time, I would often draw, paint, listen to my parents' collection of rock & roll records, or, as I entered my teens, play guitar and sing. Through my high school years I had a lot of fun learning to play the songs I heard on the radio, playing in the church choir and performing in the odd variety show. During my undergraduate years, I was a hit at parties where we would drunkenly reproduce hit songs from the past decades. Music would eventually become the other defining pillar of my identity.

By the time I was 24 and just around the corner from my 'snap', I was beginning to explore songwriting. Writing my own songs was something I never had thought I could do, and to take the plunge into creating music out of thin air was exhilarating. The high of finishing my first song in the sunny stillness of my kitchen is something that I will never forget, a high that I will probably continue to chase until I die. I felt I was growing and developing new talents. But other things were happening too...

Just as my Master's thesis research was getting off the ground, I was becoming disillusioned with science.

For one thing, I was beginning to realize that the further you went in scientific endeavour, the smaller your area of focus became. My own research was quite specialized – I was studying how muscle fibres were activated during different speeds and intensities of bicycle riding – and it seemed that many scientists' work was focused on increasingly smaller pieces of the big picture. I was seeing that there were highly esteemed people out there who knew volumes about rat mitochondrial DNA but probably couldn't tell you much about nutrition or psychology. I was questioning whether cutting the world up into smaller and smaller pieces was an effective way of getting to a greater truth.

In addition, I had just taken a course in research methods in which we had discussed the human elements of science, including the shocking cases of fraud in science. (Did you know that the results of Gregor Mendel's famous round/ wrinkled pea genetics experiment may have been 'cooked' to appear better than they actually were? Yeah, me neither.) In my naivety, I hadn't even considered that there were egos, politics and a 'star' system in science, and that some people would do anything – literally lie, cheat and steal – to get ahead in the game. Despite all the checks and balances, fraud makes its way into publication with alarming frequency. How could I trust such a system?

Simultaneously, I was becoming disillusioned with my narrow understanding of 'God'. Having left my cocoon of small-town-mindedness, I was learning about other religions, philosophies and, most intriguing to my expanding mind, psychedelic drugs.

To give some perspective, this was in the early days of the Internet as we know it. We had just left behind the world of monochromatic, text-only, cathode-ray-tube monitors and moved into the first graphical user interface operating systems. Bulletin board systems (BBS) were making way for search engines and HTML. There was very little censoring of information, like there was on TV or in public libraries. For the first time in history, almost anything you would ever want to know about LSD, magic mushrooms and other psyche-delics was freely available at the touch of a button. While we don't even bat an eyelash at this today, back then, it was a consciousness revolution.

As you can imagine, being a teachers' kid, I did not have any experience with drugs in my youth. In my early 20s I used alcohol and tried a little cannabis, but nothing else. However, the Internet was providing an intriguing view of psychedelic drugs as a means of exploring both our own minds and our connection to external reality, in a way that objective science and dogmatic religion never could. I was entranced. I was particularly interested in how psychedelic compounds had a way of connecting one with a sense of universal consciousness, a state known as ego-death where all sense of individual selfhood is stripped away, giving way to a blissful connection with 'all that there is'. There was no escapism in my desire to 'kill' my ego. For the most part (at this time), I liked myself and my life. I was not depressed or self-loathing. I just wanted to experience an intense connec-tion with whatever was *out there* – God, Spirit, the Universe, Unity Consciousness, whatever you want to call it.

But for me, the shy kid with a lot of 'square' friends, I was: 1) too scared and 2) lacking the resources to go out and score some acid or psilocybe mushrooms. So I read...a lot. I read Timothy Leary and Terence McKenna and Aldous Huxley and Ken Kesey. I read about the 1960s hippie and music scenes. I read about rave culture. I read how Alexan-der Shulgin invented more psychoactive tryptamines and phenethylamines than I could even keep straight in my head.

And I schemed several ways to try to get where I wanted without going down the rabbit hole of *insert ominous music here*...illegal drugs. I tried all sorts of legal plants, such as nutmeg and kava root, but they were more relaxing than mind-altering. Finally, I came upon 'Heavenly Blue' morning glory seeds. These contain lysergic acid amide, a close cousin to LSD (they also are often treated with poison to dissuade people from taking them internally, so proceed with caution). One day, I got up the courage and went down to my local garden centre and bought 3 packets of these babies. After some reading, a little meditation and a few deeps breaths to calm my nerves, down the hatch they went. I paid the ticket, as they say, and now I was waiting for the ride.

And waiting.

And waiting.

After an hour or more I decided that either it wasn't going to happen or it needed a little jump start to get things going. So I smoked some cannabis. Bad idea. Within minutes I was on the most terrifying ride of my life. A two-hour long panic attack-slash-guilt trip at full throttle. I held on white-knuckled as my heart raced, my brain replayed the worst things I ever did and my vision did circles like a clothes dryer on, well, acid. Nothing could have prepared me for the fear that I went through that day.

And yet *plot twist*, this is not what made me snap. In fact, I was all the more intrigued. If a combination of plants could so radically alter my mind so quickly, I wondered, what else was my mind capable of, and what are the purposes of every-day consciousness and so-called altered states of reality?

To make a long story short, I did find what I was looking for, in a sense. A few years later, I learned to grow psilocybe mushrooms and had a 'breakthrough experience' where I lost my ego, communed with Spirit and bathed in the bliss of eternal consciousness. It was breathtakingly beautiful and profound. The beginning of the trip was rough, but I expected and anticipated this due to my prior education and rode the *Bardos,* as they are known in Tibetan Buddhism, through to the unconditional love, light and unity on the other side. It was easily one of the most profound experiences of my life.

But taking psychedelics and getting to an 'enlightened' state is the easy part. The hard part is integrating what you experience back into everyday life. And this, my friends, is what made me snap. I wasn't ready to apply this joyous experience to my waking life.

So here I was, a disgruntled scientist-in-training with a religious background who had just discovered my ability to express myself artistically through songwriting, and had just visited the Light with a large dose of mushrooms. Previously, my world had been primarily defined by objectivity, sprinkled with a little faith. Theories were tested by the gathering of evidence via the scientific method, and the results of these experiments were freely disseminated and allowed to be tested by other scientists to determine the most statistically probable explanations for the 'stuff' happening around and to us. Added to that, there may or may not be a higher power that kinda makes the gears in this stuff work, and if we look deep enough we might one day find evidence of God, too.

Right...but now, not only was I starting to believe that

objectivity was impossible (even quantum physicists were suggesting that the act of observing could alter the behaviour of subatomic particles), but I also wondered if immersing myself in the subjective experience of life and making art about inner truths would be more a meaningful quest. I was not the type, however, to wildly change direction and dive into making music as my primary obsession. I was too 'sensible' for that. So, I kept my feet in both ponds, finishing my Master's degree and eventually teaching exercise science on one hand while exploring consciousness, spirituality and music on the other, all the while desperately searching for the meaning behind it all.

I didn't realize it then, but I also had a bit of a Messiah complex. I saw suffering in the world, and I wanted to solve the puzzle of 'life, the universe and everything' so that I could help people. But the more I looked, the more frustrated I became. I needed the whole answer, not just little pieces. Rather than humbly learning, developing strong habits and bettering myself every day, I put myself through a perfection-ist, ego-driven torture to find some sort of ultimate truth and save the world.

Over time, I began to hate my job, avoid people and spend increasing amounts of time in bed, hating myself. There were days that I would drive toward my university office but not be able to turn into the driveway. Instead, I would drive for hours in anxious self-examination, trying desperately to force my work ethic to overpower my existential dread.

Even the birth of my only daughter didn't pull me com-pletely out of my personal hell (though eventually, I believe she had a great deal to do with saving me). My relationship with my wife deteriorated and I turned increasingly to alcohol and other non-psychedelic drugs to numb myself. Let's just say that the end of my 20s and a good portion of my 30s were not very joyful overall.

This book, however, is not a story about one man's descent to rock bottom. I'm not going to talk about my struggles with alcohol, my slide into depression, my toxic self-obsession or my low self-worth. Some people get a guilty little thrill out of reading such stories because it makes them feel a bit better about themselves. I am not here to make you feel better by talking about my years down in the mud.

What I *am* going to share with you is what I learned in the dozen or so years after I started my journey out of depression and into a happier life. I am going to share with you anecdotes about myself and others carving out a more joyful existence. And I am going to share with you real, practical tools that can help you find more joy.

I am writing this book because, over the years of recovering from depression and building a more joyful life, I have come to understand that there are certain easily-applied principles that can help you to create a more joyful life for yourself, regardless of your current circumstances. I am writing this so that you can take a much more direct route to joy than the fumbling, meandering, often painful route that I took over the span of a decade. There may not be magic pills or shortcuts, but getting to a sustainable sense of joy may be a whole lot easier than you think!

chapter 1

Have You Heard the Good News About Joy?

Joy, happiness, contentment, pleasure. We use these words somewhat interchangeably, but we do sense nuances between them as well, and those nuances might be different for different people or in various contexts. However, I think the distinctions between these and other words we use to describe positive feelings come down mostly to the *intensity* and *duration* of those feelings. For example, we might use 'pleasure' to describe a sensation that is intense and short-lived, whereas 'happiness' might be a milder but longer-lasting emotion. 'Contentment' is usually seen as another step lower in intensity and brings images of calmness, like a cat after a saucer of milk in front of a fireplace. Contentment may be seen in our Western society as too passive. If you are content, perhaps you are not hungry enough to pursue your goals and aspirations. In American popular culture, 'happiness' is the most prevalent term for describing positive emotions, and 'the pursuit of happiness' is a near-sacred value and the default mode of operation. Happiness seems to be what we are all after.

But what about 'joy'? How is joy set apart from the other positive emotions? I consider joy to be somewhat more intense than happiness and possibly, but not necessarily, shorter-lived. I suspect most people see joy as more fleeting than happiness, but as we continue, I will attempt to show you that joy—that deeper more intense version of happiness—can actually be sustainable!

I would also say that 'joy' has a more *spiritual* connotation than happiness. This is perhaps why some people are a little nervous to embrace the concept of joy. The word 'joy' is probably used most in organized religion. As such, for many people, 'joy' brings to mind a kind of naive, doe-eyed belief, in which one sees unicorns pooping rainbows even while standing knee-deep in horse shit. This is why many of us cross the street when we see a pair of grinning young men wearing white shirts, black ties and name tags and carrying a book. After all, we live in a world where there is tremendous injustice, corruption, conflict and suffering. How can we truly be joyful on a consistent basis when there is such strife? (And why would a loving and awesome God allow this shit to happen, anyway?) We will dive into that question a little bit later, but simply put, I think when someone comes to a deeper, spiritual understanding of the dualities of our three-dimensional existence, they come to realize that great happiness and great joy can exist alongside deep pain, and it is in fact our suffering that makes our joys more meaningful than if we lived in a constant state of blissful unicorn poop.

So for the purposes of this book, here are some ways that I distinguish happiness and joy:

- Joy is deeper than happiness – if happiness is 'like', then joy is 'love.'
- Joy is spicier (I considered entitling this book *Sriracha for Your Soul!*).
- Joy is much more in the present, whereas happiness can be past, present or future ('I was so happy back then' or 'I'll be so happy when I get married').
- Joy is less dependent on circumstances (e.g., finances, relationship status, career satisfaction), whereas happiness is often based upon such conditions.
- Due to its more spiritual nature, joy is more likely to be connected to selflessness, gratitude and accomplishment, whereas happiness can come from any pleasant experience (you might be happy after having a good meal at a restaurant, but more joyful after cooking a home-made meal for a friend who had a rough day).

As you may be starting to realize, in addition to our pursuit of happiness, we would be well-served to try to bring more joy into our lives as well. In fact, focusing more on joy may actually help us to get to happiness more quickly and easily than if we thought only about our happiness.

One final note about our society's perception of the word 'joy,' and this one is for the fellas mostly. In addition to being seen as having a religious connotation, the idea of 'joy' might be a little uncomfortable for the more macho, old-school men out there. In our cultural past, men were expected to be stoic and non-emotional, so the word 'joy' might come off as a little bit, you know, frou-frou. But here's the thing: joy is mostly internal, and completely individual. To be joyful doesn't mean you have to be gushing with adolescent girl bubbliness all the time. Let me assure you, you can live in joy and still be a hard-nosed, ass-kicking SOB. That goes for the ladies and non-binary folks, too.

chapter 2

Happily Ever After

O nce upon a time, there lived a young person who had a very ordinary life, or if it was in any way extraordinary it was extraordinarily bad. And it would only get worse. They were picked on, ostracized, harassed. Their safety, community, and even their very life were threatened by the most evil of foes! This young person faced trials and tribulations that would kill weaker individuals, crossing great divides, physical and emotional, to face monsters and demons, external and internal. In a thrilling, mortal showdown, they finally slayed the 'dragons' of their enormous torment. Having vanquished these evil foes, the young hero won the heart of their true love, and they lived...happily ever after.

So goes almost every well-known fairy tale.

Now, the thing about fairy tales is that we know they are not reality. Or at least, our ancestors did. (They are useful metaphors to be certain, but still not reality.) Then TV and movies came along, and we won't name any names here, but some really creative people brought these fairy tales to life in fantastic and compelling ways. As children growing up in the cinematic and multimedia age, how many of these movies did we watch? How many promises were made to us of happily-ever-after, if only we got the house, the spouse, the right job? And this fairy tale formula extends well beyond childhood movies. Even into adulthood, the formulas in many adventure, fantasy, superhero and romantic comedy movies are thinly veiled fairy tales. How have our views on happiness been skewed by these stories, which in the old days were acknowledged to be pollyannaish, ridiculously optimistic exaggerations of real life? Obviously, we should know that even after we get married, have kids and develop our dream career, life is still going to be gritty and challenging and imperfect—shouldn't we?

I believe that at a certain level, we unfortunately internalize the fantasy of 'happily ever after,' to the detriment of our long-term happiness. You don't have to search far to find an Internet meme or piece of inspirational kitsch home decor that proclaims that happiness is a journey, not a destination. And yet, actually embracing the journey of happiness (which is more like joyfulness) seems to be more difficult than the 'live, love, laugh' tole painting would suggest.

Part of the issue might be our thinking around goal-setting and achievement.

Let me say first that I am a huge proponent of having well-defined, attainable and challenging goals over different time frames and multiple facets of your life. I think that the majority of people who are living joyful lives are goal-setters and high achievers. However, making the achievement of our goals a *condition* for our happiness is a big mistake. The people who are most joyful take joy and pride in the journey and process of working toward goals, rather than the achievement. They find joy within the work itself, and realize that conditional happiness is actually a trap that can lead to perpetual unhappiness. Even as goals are achieved, we can be left unsatisfied, chasing the next thing that we think will bring us 'happily-ever-after.'

Let's take a hypothetical example to see how this works: Trina and Joanne are both in their twenties and both have the goal of becoming an executive at a Fortune 500 company by the age of thirty. The difference in their thinking is that Trina will be unhappy, to the point of being miserable, until she reaches that goal, whereas Joanne maintains an underlying feeling of deep joy while working toward her goal. Joanne may not be *satisfied* until she becomes an exec, but she chooses to be happy, enjoying the ride. Who do you think has a better shot at reaching their goal? Who leads a more fulfilling existence?

Let me tell you, misery can actually be a great motivator. So in that sense, Trina may actually have as good a chance or maybe even better than Joanne, I don't know. Joanne may have a better chance because her performance is better as a result of her joy. There may not be a clear answer to that.

But who do you think has a richer life on the way to their goal? And how will they feel after they reach the goal? My guess is that Joanne will celebrate her victory, bask in the joy of achievement for an appropriate amount of time, and then shift her focus to the next set of goals, creating a cascade of fulfillment and advancement. Trina may also have a honeymoon period with her new job, but over time she may become disillusioned and wonder why she is not happy with her achievement. She too may set new goals, but rather than being an easy cascade, it will be a treadmill of chasing happiness, or a high that never comes despite external achievement.

And what if they don't reach their goal? Someone like Joanne might be more likely to see this failure as a learning experience and move forward. Her inner joy is not jeopardized, because she is not attached to the specific outcome. Of course, she is disappointed that she did not reach her goal, but she uses it as fuel in a healthy way to continue the good fight. She refocuses, re-frames her goal, and moves on.

Trina, on the other hand, may be utterly shattered by her unrealized goal. She has been miserable for years chasing this dream, and she failed. This is a disaster piled on top of an already miserable existence.

The difference in these two women's ways of life is primarily one of attitude. It may seem trite to say that a more joyful life is a choice, but to an extent it is. After many years of feeling stuck in a depression that clouded practically every moment of my life, I made a *conscious choice* to never live that way again. And while I may still have the odd down day (as everyone does), I have stayed true to that choice. Even during times of great sadness, grief or anger, I know that there is a 'core' of unshakable joy deep down inside me. If you're taking notes, this is the one concept I wish for everyone to take away from this book—even when circumstances are difficult, you CAN have an unshakable joy deep inside, waiting for you to return to it! I believe that no matter how far away our goals are, we will arrive at them sooner and with our hearts in better condition if we choose to value joy and work on creating and maintaining that core, much like Joanne did in the example above.

—⁘—

This basic concept can apply to all areas of our lives, including career, money, possessions, health, friendships and hobbies. Not surprisingly, though, the area of life that most often falls prey to happily-ever-after syndrome is romantic relationships. After all, that's the message behind a lot of those fairy tales, right? And for good reason, too. We know that our DNA is programmed to make us do all sorts of crazy things in the name of propagating itself. The drive toward reproducing is the strongest urge that we have, and tends to drive a lot of our other urges. We work at making money, for example, not just for the freedom it affords us, but also, consciously or unconsciously, to make us more attractive to prospective mates by demonstrating our capability to support and raise children. Therefore, it shouldn't be a shocker that many of us are miserable when we are single, and assume that all our problems will be over and life will be grand once we finally find Mx. Right.

Let's not dismiss the wonderful and magical fulfillment that deep loving relationships and raising a family can bring. I would argue that bringing children into the world with someone that you love may be one of the greatest, if not the greatest, joy that anyone can aspire to. However, as with our career example, the pursuit of that ideal can be anything but joyful if you choose not to be happy until you are in the perfect marriage with the perfect 2.5 kids, dog and picket fence.

The extent to which our society's narratives around romance affect girls and their self-image is particularly disturbing. In the 1950s, women were explicitly encouraged to aspire to be the perfect housewife and little more. While much has changed since then, cultural messages still insinuate that girls' dreams will come true once they 'get that ring on their finger.' And we only have to look at the divorce statistics to realize this is a fantasy. People who fall for these distorted cultural messages often fail to notice how much hard work, communication, respect and trust are required to maintain a quality relationship. 'Happily-ever-after in love' is sold to girls as a panacea for sadness, and it is doing them a disservice.

One of the tools I use in my wellness practise is Tarot. I use the lessons contained in the Tarot deck to help people navigate life's challenges, make decisions and deepen their spiritual understanding. In the past few years, Tarot has become increasingly popular among young people, and I often read for teenage girls and young women. I have found it unsettling how many of these young people are focused on—sometimes even obsessed with—finding and keeping a romantic partner. More than occasionally, this focus on attaching themselves to another person comes at the expense of their personal development and other relationships. An obsession with being partnered at too young an age can actually set up unhealthy patterns, such as co-dependence, because they are trying to force themselves into love before they have developed their own persona, self-esteem and self-love. As RuPaul says, 'If you can't love yourself, how in the hell you gonna love somebody else?' It seems to me that dating as a teenager should be fun, light and balanced within a context of self-discovery. Maybe save the 'old ball and chain' for later in life!

Even for people in their twenties and beyond, there is a good lesson in this. Like our joyful career vixen Joanne, those who focus on creating self-love, joy and development in their own life are in a far better position to attract the love of their life than those who wallow in the misery of being single. With solid self-esteem and positive life skills under their belt, when their soulmate comes along, they are far more likely to be able to develop a healthy partnered life with that person. So many people who hold the dream of happily-ever-after actually end up being miserable in their marriages, because it is not the fairy tale they held it up to be in their fantasies. But becoming a whole, healthy person, rather than looking for someone to 'complete you,' is actually a far better approach to a successful relationship. And *even better* than just becoming a whole healthy person, is enjoying the scenery while you get to that whole, healthy place, and organically attracting that soul mate who makes your already awesome life even more amazing.

No matter what your goals are, finding and celebrating the joy of the process really is everything. As a final illustration of this, let me tell you about a small moment that seems insignificant but is charged with joyful meaning. First, let me tell you that the vast majority of the time when I go running, I push myself and I am rather goal-focused. But I'm also not at all drudging through miserably. There is a kind of joy to the madness. And occasionally, I will stop to pet a friendly dog or check out a fantastic landscape on my way. One day, as I was on my morning run, I was immediately taken by the beauty of the forest trail I was running on. I stopped for five or ten seconds and just took it in, breathing in the living wonder of the trees, grasses and wildflowers. Inwardly, I kinda laughed, because the phrase 'stop and smell the roses' came into my mind. I'm still hellbent on achieving better fitness, well-being and clearer thinking. I am unwaveringly focused on my goals, but I am en- JOY-ing the journey on my way to my 'happily-ever-after.'

chapter 3

Choose Joy

I f you're like me (and the fact that you're reading this tells me it's likely), you've probably read a ton of personal development books. If so, good for you! Some have possibly impacted your life in tremendous ways. Others may have provided you with the odd 'life hack' or a bit of wisdom that has stuck with you throughout the years. Others still may not have left you with any concrete skills, but nevertheless inspired or motivated you to begin to live your life differently. (Hopefully this book will fulfill at least some or all of the above!)

While each personal development book has its own unique subjects, philosophy and approaches, there is increasingly one concept that is fundamental to the vast majority of these books. Whether it's about making more money or becoming more organized or finding your dream career, the first and by far the most important step is to fiercely and unequivocally make the *choice* to do it.

When I was depressed, spending way too many hours in bed and thinking about ending it all, there came a time when I said 'enough is enough'. I remember it clearly. I had been on anti-depressant medication for about a year-and-a-half. I was barely keeping my head above water. I had a young daughter and it seemed even the wonder of seeing her grow was not inspiring me to anything. I was phoning it in as a parent. I knew I was, and that made me feel even more horrible. My music career was floundering and my relationships were shallow. I was a walking zombie.

Then that day came where I stood up and said 'I can't live like this anymore'. Right then and there, in a singular moment, I decided I was never going to be depressed again. I weaned myself off my medication, and I made certain that no matter how difficult my circumstances or how sad or angry I was in a particular time period, I was not going to wallow in negative feelings, catastrophize my feelings, become over-dramatic or self-indulgent. I decided that life was too short for depression and I chose not to be.

And for the most part, I have succeeded in that.

Actor and musician Will Smith once said in an interview, 'There's a redemptive power that making a choice has... Rather than feeling like you're an effect to all the things that are happening, make a choice! Right? Just decide what it's gonna be, who you're gonna be, how you are going to do it. Just decide. And from that point, the universe is going to get out of your way.'

Choice is one of the most powerful tools we have. Just as you can choose to not be depressed, choose to be a baker rather than a banker, choose to style your hair a certain way, or choose to go to the movies on Friday night, you can also choose to be joyful!

It's worth reading again. *You can choose to be joyful.*

Now, you may be saying, 'Wait. I can't control my thoughts and emotions! What about when I get up out of bed on Monday morning and it's cold and I'm cranky and the cat puked on the rug and I'm going to be late for work?' Well, let me ask you this...if you can't control your thoughts and emotions, who is controlling them for you? This may seem like a glib or even ridiculous question, but it is worth thinking about. It makes sense that we should be in control of our thoughts all, or at least most, of the time. And yet, our brain is wired such that we have a certain amount of auto-pilot. Otherwise, we literally might not even be able to walk and chew gum at the same time. The danger is that many people go too deep into auto-pilot mode, to the point where they are truly having their thoughts and emotions controlled by their environment. Events, conditions, other people's opinions and indeed media (advertisements, television, social media, and the like) can influence people's minds to such an extent that they feel that they have no choice but to be miserable. After all, the news is always gloomy—everyone is just out for themselves, hurricane season is coming, Instagram influencers have much more glamorous lives, and on and on...

If that is our default mode of thinking, how can we even consider joy? And again, who is controlling our thoughts?

I feel that the choice to be joyful is really a combination of two concepts. I will introduce them here, and then dive deeper into each of them later in the book, because I think they are two of the true pillars of a joyful and successful life: mindfulness and gratitude.

Mindfulness is basically being aware and conscious of the present moment, and calmly acknowledging our thoughts, emotions and bodily sensations. It is an idea that is very much in vogue among growth-minded people today (and for good reason), but it's the Buddha who is considered the ancient authority on mindfulness. In Buddhism, mindfulness is just one of the steps of the Noble Eightfold Path, a set of practises that is meant to lead one to liberation from the painful cycles of death and rebirth. Buddha taught that to be mindful, one should pay 'bare attention' to one's body, emotions, thoughts and phenomena.

Today, in the modern Western world, our understanding of mindfulness is much more basic than the Buddhist view. It is largely taken on its own merits, as opposed to being one aspect of a larger system of values and practises, and it is focused on the self as opposed to the 'non-self' of Buddhism. Still, many people today are discovering the benefits of paying closer attention to their thoughts and feelings. This is a first step to being able to 'groom' your thoughts and emotions so that you can go through life with more positivity, more gratitude and indeed more joy. I call it 'mind gardening'!

When you tend a garden, you are trying to selectively nurture the plants that are useful to you, like veggies and flowers, while minimizing the appearance and growth of plants that are not useful and compete with your good plants for resources, known as weeds. I think you know where I'm going with this metaphor, but consider that when plants are just sprouting and in their infancy, it can be quite difficult to tell a wanted plant from a weed. You have to pay very close attention. However, the earlier you weed a garden, the easier it is to stay ahead of the weed pressure throughout a growing season. So, a smart gardener will get down to weeding as soon as they can clearly identify the shoots of their wanted plants.

Now, apply this to your mind. People who are not mindful of their thought patterns can get pretty far down a rabbit hole of nasty, weedy thoughts before they even realize they are even in a hole. By the time they realize something is wrong, their mental garden is overrun with weeds, to the point where they may need a mental health professional to help them untangle the healthy, wanted thought patterns from the unhealthy ones.

As opposed to this unhealthy mind overrun with 'weeds', the mindful intelligence monitors itself regularly by being calmly aware and accepting of its own thoughts and patterns. Therefore, the owner of this mindful mind is more able to catch unhealthy thoughts and deal with them before they become problematic, and thus keep a healthy mind-garden where productive thoughts bloom and thrive.

Now, again, I don't mean to say that we can forever live in a state of unending bliss, where nothing bothers us in our happy little bubble. I am not suggesting that so-called 'negative' thoughts and emotions have no place in our mind. That would not be healthy, either. As I write this, an uncle of mine has just passed after a difficult and painful battle with cancer. I, of course, am sad and grieving. This is a healthy expression of thoughts and feelings that are difficult because of an unhappy circumstance. However, in my carefully tended mind-garden, I will not, for example, let those feelings lead me down a path of thinking that life is cruel and meaning-less. Rather, I grieve and sit with my sadness for my cousins who lost their dad, but also celebrate the life they had with him and all the things that he accomplished in his life. I take time to think about how death, although tremendously painful, mysterious and frightening, actually motivates us and gives life a profound meaning that would not exist if we lived forever.

This is pretty deep talk, but it is an example of how, the more we practise paying close attention to our thoughts and feelings, the more we can then shape the way we think and live our life more purposefully, rather than being at the whim of our 'auto-pilot'.

At this point, you may be thinking, *'But how do I get there?'* And yes, mindfulness is a journey rather than a des-tination. Buddhist monks practise for decades to reach states of enlightenment. But I believe that, with just a few months of conscious effort, you can start to be much more in control of your thought patterns. In Chapter 10, we will look at some specific strategies for improving your mindfulness. However, the main tool most people use to attempt to become more mindful is meditation.

When most people think of meditation, they think about trying to quiet their mind, with the goal to not have any thoughts at all. While this type of meditation has its place, it is not mindfulness meditation, and it can be extremely frus-trating for beginners. A better place to start with meditation, and one that is more suited to cultivating mindfulness, is simply to sit quietly with your thoughts and try to maintain a bit of detachment from them. It is often described as observing your thoughts as if they were floating on a river. You pay attention to what comes into your mind, take note of it and then let it go as it floats on down the river.

Once you have practised this type of meditation for a while, say a few months, and are comfortable with it, you can then try a meditation which is more of a focusing of attention, where you try to hold a particular thought or feeling for as long as possible. When you notice your mind starting to wander, take note as you did before and let the intrusive thought or feeling go, returning to your point of focus. This really helps to build control over your thoughts and feelings, and allows you to shift your general focus to joy-promoting emotions, such as gratitude.

Gratitude is the second concept that is crucial to being able to *choose* a more joyful life. It is one of the most powerful emotions for creating not only more joy, but also more success and fulfillment. For me, starting a mindful gratitude practise (which has evolved over the years, but basically involves consciously being more grateful and sitting with the feeling of gratitude as often as possible) is one of the top three things I have done in my life to improve my overall well-being.

Many authors and speakers have talked about the power of gratitude to bring more good things into our lives. One the most influential of these in recent years has been Rhonda Byrne, the author of *The Secret* series of books and films. Like many readers, I was initially drawn to the series by the promise of attracting more abundance into my life. The first two books focus on holding on to the feeling of already having what it is you desire, and being grateful for what you already have and will have in the future. The aim is to shift your energetic frequency to one that attracts abundance, prosperity and your dream life. There are many hard-core believers of this philosophy, and just as many skeptics. I honestly didn't know what to think of it when I first encountered it, but I suspended my disbelief and went about trying to shift my mindset to one of feeling abundant and grateful.

Now, let's just say that practising gratitude, in and of itself, hasn't made me rich beyond my wildest dreams or gotten me a huge record deal (yet!). To paraphrase Jim Carrey, you can't just put in your order to the universe and then sit back and have a sandwich. You still have to do the work. However, the changes that have developed in my mood, attitude, energy and relationships have been nothing less than amazing. And these changes have gone a long way to making my life better. (And yes, my career and financial situation have certainly improved over where they were five years ago, thank you very much!)

A critical part of this type of gratitude practise is to feel grateful not only for the things and circumstances that we already have but also for those that we would like to have. Being thankful for things in advance gets us in the state of mind of having them already. This not only helps us to realize that we deserve them but also primes our mental attitude for the state of possession. It makes it real. People who espouse the law of attraction philosophy advise us to do things that make our dream seem tangible to our senses. If you want a house in a certain neighbourhood, go to open houses there. If you want a certain kind of car, go test drive one and take your picture in it (even if you can't currently afford it). If you want a job at a certain office, go eat lunch at the café next door once a week. If you want a romantic partner, put out another place setting at dinner. (OK, that one may feel a little silly to you, but go for it! Nobody's watching.) And while you are doing these things, bask in the feeling of gratitude because your dream has been fulfilled.

Gratitude, like mindfulness, is something that you get better at over time, and eventually it becomes part of your nature. When gratitude and mindfulness become as natural as breathing, then you are in a perfect position to choose joy in your life. You are mindfully gardening your thoughts and being grateful for all the joyful things in your life, and so you practically have no choice but to have more joy!

Once again, this may all seem like it's too good to be true, or that I am offering a magic pill that will immediately catapult you into state of bliss just by making a simple decision. This isn't really the case. It takes a bit of work to acquire the mental discipline to focus on being more joyful, but once you gain some momentum, it becomes much easier to hold on to the state of joy more and more consistently. And really, when you consider the alternative of being miserable, why wouldn't you want to put in that little bit of effort?

Now, this brings up another important point, which is that our moods and emotions are somewhat influenced by our physiology and subconscious processes. Even for those of us who are in decent health and maintain positive attitudes, it can be very difficult to be joyful when we are physically exhausted, in pain or suffering from biochemical imbalances. Believe me, I know what it's like to try being upbeat and friendly when you're running on minimal sleep, nursing a monster headache, and dealing with all the other aches, pains and stresses that come with being a human. Hormones such as estrogen, testosterone, oxytocin, cortisol and vasopressin, and neurotransmitters like dopamine and serotonin are also involved in co-creating our emotional states and moods. However, I think that our knowledge of these chemical systems in our bodies has led many of us to feel as though we are prisoners of our own biochemistry. The fact is that it's a two-way street. Your thoughts and habits can actually alter your hormone and neurotransmitter levels, just as they can influence your emotions. It's somewhat like the old chicken-and-egg riddle. Are you miserable because your body isn't making enough dopamine? Or is your body not making enough dopamine because you are miserable? The answer is probably a little bit of both – after all, you are an extremely dynamic being! However, I believe very strongly that our beliefs, attitudes and habits are what create our internal reality. You can change your biochemical profile by changing your thoughts and actions.

The positive attitude of a disciplined mind, combined with a healthy diet and exercise, make it darn near impossible to stay stuck in a hormonal soup of doom and gloom for very long. OK, for some people, the thought of eating vegetables and working out may not seem very joyful. But is the routine of snacking on potato chips and soda while binge-watching Netflix really happiness? Occasionally, sure it is. I love a good veg session in front of a movie from time to time. But in the long run, finding and focusing on nutritious foods that you love and activities that make you feel alive and vibrant are going to go much further toward joyfulness than indulging in processed junk food on the couch.

Then, the two-way street really starts to boost your vibration to a new level. You are practising mindful gratitude (a.k.a. choosing joy), and your healthy habits are supporting your mind and body to make you feel physically and emotionally better, in turn making it easier to think positively and choose joy. It's an upward spiral!

chapter 4

A Time for Joy

'To everything there is a season, and a time to every purpose under the heaven: A time to be born, and a time to die...' So begins one of the more recognizable verses of Ecclesiastes in the Old Testament. Unless we figure out a way around it, time as we know it moves only in one direction, and we as human beings move from birth toward death. In this framework of time marching on, we recognize three divisions of time: the past, which has already occurred, the future which has yet to occur, and the present, which is a knife's edge slice of the now, always moving and yet eternal in its 'nowness'.

In our last chapter, we looked at mindfulness, and one aspect of mindfulness, especially in the Western understanding of it, is being present in the 'now'. By this I mean having *most* of our attention focused on the present. It would be impossible and irresponsible to have all of our attention on the present constantly – after all, we must recognize and benefit from the lessons of our past, and plan for our future. However, being centered in the present moment is a beneficial mental habit that cultivates an environment befitting joy.

Being too focused on the past or on the future can cause us to literally miss out on things that are happening right in front of our faces. Back in the 1990s, I was getting ready to go see the Canadian rock band Trooper in concert (I'm cringing at it now, but at the time I was pretty excited), and like many other concert-goers, I partook in some cannabis—a little too much cannabis. For me at the time, over-indulging would cause me to become very anxious and guilt-ridden, and I often spiralled into stressful states of beating myself up about my past. I would feel like a horrible person and tear apart in minute detail all the supposedly bad things I did throughout my life. It was the opposite of mindfully living in the present moment. To make a long story short, I did not enjoy the concert. In fact, I spent a good portion of it in a back corner practically hyperventilating and holding my head in my hands, living in the past.

Of course, that example was plant-medicine-induced, but it is a good lesson for how we may be missing out on cool things because our minds are immersed in the past or the future. Are you stressing out over Monday's staff meeting while at your child's soccer game on Saturday? Reliving past hurts or mistakes while at the family potluck? Spending that gorgeous day at the beach thinking about the looming tax deadline?

Being conscious and deliberate about how much time we are spending present in the 'now', while also planning for the future and examining the past is another form of mind-gardening that can help us grow more joyful. How much time you spend in each mode is up to you, but I would suggest that the happier and more successful people in the world spend the vast majority of their time focused on the present and the future.

This approach is like a more nuanced version of time management. When you manage your time well, you have a fair amount of control over how much time you devote to things you need and want to do. You balance your needs and wants with those of your family, employers/employees/ clients and friends. You allot time for work/passions/purpose, family/community and recreation/self-care. But when you are also mindfully conscious of the time you spend, you ensure that you are as fully present as possible for each of these activities and people.

There are some celebrities and other high-achievers who, no matter who they are with—whether another celebrity or an 'ordinary' person on the street—are totally engaged and present with that person. Maybe you've heard about or even met someone like this. It feels good, doesn't it, to be in the presence of a person like that? Likewise, it feels good to be completely engaged and present yourself. That is a special type of mindfulness, and it comes with knowing that there is 'a time for everything under heaven'. I occasionally facilitate guided meditation sessions, and when we are beginning the meditation, decompressing and focusing on breathing, I often tell my participants to imagine themselves in a room with a trunk over in the corner. I tell them to imagine themselves opening the trunk, putting all their worries inside and closing the lid. Then I say, 'They will be safe there. If you still want them when we're done you can pick them up!'

So, how do you garden your mind so that you can focus on the present when you want, the future when you want and the past when you want?

Again, meditation is a great way to begin this process. Try meditating as we did in Chapter 3, just focusing on your breath for a few minutes and then sitting with your thoughts, 'watching' them go by. When you notice you've gone down a path of thinking a certain series of thoughts, stop and ask yourself, 'Was I thinking about the past, present or future?' Take note of what 'tense' your thoughts were in and then let them go, returning to focus on your breath, and then see what your mind settles on next. When you notice the next line of thinking taking place, check what tense you've been thinking in, make note of it, then let the thoughts go and continue.

Once you have practised this for a while in quiet meditation, you might even start to notice yourself doing this in the course of an average day. This is where the real magic starts to happen. When you realize that you've been subconsciously getting lost in an unwanted thought pattern and you begin to consciously change course earlier and earlier in your 'autopilot' state, you are on the road to the kind of mental discipline that can make big changes in your life.

A few words here about the concept of mental discipline. The word 'discipline' has, understandably, a negative connotation for a lot of people. Especially as children, we equate discipline with punishment because we don't know any better, and frankly some of the adults in our lives don't know any better either, and try to enforce discipline in a heavy-handed, militaristic manner. As small children we explore the world in sometimes wild, undisciplined ways because we haven't learned the cause-and-effect laws of our four-dimensional, earthly reality. If it weren't for our parents, we might put our hand in a fire or toddle off a cliff or drown in a foot of water. Then, through our childhood and adolescence, we learn to discipline our behaviour and our thoughts, still mostly through positive and negative feedback from adults, so that we can better navigate the physical and social world we live in. But sometimes, when we 'leave the nest', we choose to let slip, or even rebel against, disciplines that were imposed on us. A kid who was forced to do pull-ups in gym class might avoid exercise for years. A kid whose parents demanded excellent grades in school might turn out to be anti-intellectual in adulthood. Even worse, kids who are subjected to abuse as opposed to loving discipline often end up with innumerable forms of dissociative and destructive coping mechanisms, leading to addiction, mental illness and self-harming.

And so, the term 'mental discipline' might rub some people the wrong way—as dull or painful or self-flagellant. But the discipline I am talking about is actually a form of self-love. I care about myself *too much* to let my mental environment be polluted by depressed, negative, self-degrading or otherwise counter-productive thoughts. (OK, I allow myself the freedom and fun of unproductive, a.k.a. *creative* thoughts a lot! But not counter-productive thoughts.) If you think of your mind as a playground for high-quality, high-vibrational thoughts, then a little bit of self-discipline and effort is a small price to pay for a massive reward!

In short, mental discipline allows us to spend the appropriate amounts of time and energy focused on the present, the future and the past. When we have a healthier relationship with time, we really start to put joy in our sights.

There is another aspect of time and our perception of it that has a tremendous implication for our well-being, happiness and joy. And well...I hate to be the bearer of bad news, but here comes the gut punch...

You are going to die.

You have an unforeseen but unquestionably finite amount of time left on this Earth.

For many people, that is frightening, and they feel that time is speeding ahead far too quickly. They want to forget about death until it barrels down upon them, hopefully a long way in the future. Of course, nobody wants to think about death too much, and it would indeed be unhealthy to obsess about it. But accepting and being mindful of our mortality can actually bring great meaning into our lives. Many may claim to want immortality, but I suspect living forever in our four-dimensional world would be a kind of hell—a meaningless, pervasive boredom. At the very least, you'd probably get awfully tired of trying to find new stuff to do after you'd mastered every sport, musical instrument, occupation and video game.

Knowing that we only have so long on this plane of exist-ence should give us motivation to give it our best shot and squeeze every bit of opportunity, love and joy out of our limited time, shouldn't it? Imagine looking back from your death bed and saying 'I know I wasn't perfect, but damn, I gave it one hell of a ride.' Doesn't that give you the ultimate reason to make the *choice*, right now, to live in joy, rather than moping around feeling sorry for yourself during this time that you have left?

I believe we should teach people to be aware and con-scious of their mortality at an early age. In Western cultures, we tend not to think about it until middle age, whereas young people can sometimes nonchalantly disregard it and float along thinking they have all the time in the world. Rather, we should take the words of Lakota Chief Low Dog to heart: 'This is a good day to die.' We never know when that time is going to come, and if we live each day like it might be our last, we are much less likely to have regrets and more likely to live in joy.

Much is to be said for the 'reconciliation of opposites', the idea that forces which appear to be opposites (light and dark, good and evil, creation and destruction, life and death) are actually complementary and interconnected. Neither can exist without the other, for if they did they would be meaningless.

Consider that maybe, just maybe, to fully enjoy life, we must actually *embrace* death. We're talking primarily about our own death here. It is much more difficult to extend this to our loved ones, of course, but even there, when we accept the possibility that the people we love may unexpectedly leave us, it can lead us to cherish even more the time that we do have with them here and now. This is not to say that death isn't sad and doesn't suck. Death is horrible. Death is messy and gross. But when we mindfully accept it as part of the miracle of creation, it makes life that much more amazing and wonderful, and something not to be sleep-walked through.

When seen in this light, where life is the interdependent counterpoint to death, living joyfully not only seems like the obvious choice, but it becomes our birthright and our destiny.

So, how do we use this to our advantage in our daily life?

This is definitely not about thinking macabre thoughts or constantly reminding yourself that you are going to shed your mortal coil someday. It's about appreciating the time you have and realizing that every moment is precious. For me, this is as simple as practising gratitude for the time that I have. This may sound a little goofy and simplistic, but... *every...single...day...* I make certain that one of the very first thoughts that I have when I wake up is, 'Thank you for this day!' It doesn't matter if I'm tired, or it's minus 20 outside, or if I have something unpleasant to do that day. I express my gratitude for the gift of today. You can do this at nighttime, too – take a few minutes before bed to review all the blessings you received during the day and be thankful for them.

Another thing that I try to do often is to contemplate the wonder of life and the world around me. Even the simplest things in nature are really miraculous when you stop to think about them. One day, as I was cooling down from my morning run, I noticed a blue jay feather on the ground and picked it up. One side of the feather's quill was subtle shades of grey and the other was a dramatic blue alternating with curved black lines. I marveled at how sharp the edge of the lines were, as if they were drawn on rather than being genetically coded into each cell of each barb of the feather. Even though I'm aware that patterns such as this likely evolved over millions of years of differentiation and mutation, I am still blown away by the mysterious intelligence that underlies life on this planet. And you and I are a part of that! We are walking, breathing miracles of creation. It may not feel like it sometimes when we are suffering, but what an honour and a privilege it is to be one of the most complex and intricate forms of intelligence in our amazing world!

When you are grateful for the time you have every single day and you maintain a sense of wonder about the world around you (keeping in mind that you yourself are a wonder), you are creating fertile ground for making the most of the time you have left in this life.

—∞—

The final time-related concept I want to talk about is quite literally connected to the title of this chapter, *A Time for Joy*. That is, making time for joy.

Earlier, we looked at how we can be more fully in the moment when joyful things are happening. For example, actively playing with your kids at that birthday party rather than going through the motions while planning your next Instagram post in your head. But what about making time for things that bring you joy? This can be one of the most challenging things for us in our fast-paced society.

For many people today, just making a living can keep us constantly in motion, frazzled and exhausted. As someone who has an entrepreneurial spirit, I often live by the maxim that I have the freedom to decide which 16 hours a day I work. OK, maybe that is a bit of an exaggeration, but the vast majority of my waking hours are spent working. Fortunately, I get great satisfaction and yes, even joy, out of my work. But for many people, between career work, housework and other obligations, it leaves very little time for anything else. Furthermore, when people who are too busy finally do get time off, some of them find themselves indulging in escapism in the form of alcohol and drugs, which in the long-term can stress the body and mind even further. At its worst, this can be a nightmarish treadmill of working hard and 'partying' hard, except that the partying is not really fun anymore and is just a road to misery.

An alternative approach is to place high value on and prioritize regenerative activities, making time for the things that light you up and feed your spirit.

I have a friend, Jack, who is a musician and songwriter. He has produced a few albums but has always had a day job unrelated to music. He has the odd paying gig, but has no ambition to make a full-time living from music, and is content to make money in other ways. For a little while a few years back, I used to pick up his son around 7:30am and drive him to work. Every day when I arrived at their house, Jack would be at his kitchen table with a cup of coffee and his guitar, practising or writing. He woke up an hour early to make time for his joy before going off to work.

I don't expect everyone will take the structured approach that Jack does, with a daily appointment at the same time, but I believe it is vitally important to carve out a bit of time every once in a while for things we deeply enjoy. True recreation has been shown time and again to make us more efficient and productive during our work time. So, making and taking time for joyful activities is in no way counter-productive to our careers. In fact, it contributes to clearer thinking, enthusiasm, efficiency and overall better performance in our working lives.

Making time in an already full schedule may seem downright impossible at times. Starting small and actually scheduling in 'me time' can be a great way to start. Adding a 15 minute interval into your calendar for your joyful activity not only encourages you to do it, but also enforces in your mind that this is an important value and a priority for you. Ultimately, you may need to establish boundaries or delegate (a.k.a. ask for help, gasp!) in order to ensure that you have time for regenerative activities, but in the long run, you will probably see that making time for joy will actually create a more balanced life that is easier to manage and more effortlessly productive.

In Chapter 1, I made the case for shifting the definition of joy a little bit. Many people see joy as a shorter, more intense burst of happiness. But I believe in viewing joy as something deeper that can be sustainable over time if we shift our attitude. That being said, long-term sustainable joy is nevertheless made up of a succession of little moments. So, making room in your life for those more intense bursts of happiness is nothing to sneeze at. Over time, if you succeed in peppering your life with as many intense joyful moments as you can manage, your overall baseline of joy can't help but go up a little, too. Thus, while we work on the mental discipline that I have been harping on about, we shouldn't forget to have some fun every once in a while! Amid the challenges and struggles that we all have, there is a beautiful, magical world that we inhabit, and it is meant for us to enjoy, so make some time and enjoy it.

chapter 5

Convenience, Comfort and Connection

I t is hard to imagine that only about a hundred and twenty years ago, the majority of households in North America did not have electricity or indoor plumbing. To get a morning coffee, one would light a gas lamp to navigate to the kitchen, stoke a wood fire in the cook stove, wait God-knows-how-long for the stove to get hot enough to boil water, go outside to hand-pump water out of the well and then finally boil the water and make coffee. Contrast that with today, when we can press a few buttons on our phone from the comfort of our bed and have a no-fat, half-foam, salted caramel latté delivered to our front door...by a robot!

Today, the average person in the 'developed' world has more convenience, comfort and connectivity than ever before. Our basic needs can usually be met with a modest job. Simple material wants are often a click or a short drive away. The comforts that were once thought to be extravagant, like designer clothes, hot tubs, golf club memberships and luxury cars, are accessible to more and more of us. And, we are able to communicate with people from across the globe at an instant from just about anywhere, on a plethora of mobile devices.

And while there is arguably much joy to be found in these marvelous comforts and conveniences that technology has brought us, we also find ourselves in a state where depression, anxiety, stress, loneliness, apathy, lack of fulfillment and burnout are so commonplace that if someone is not complaining about at least one of these afflictions, we sometimes wonder what's wrong with them. How is it that we can have so much of these 3 C's – comfort, convenience and connection – and still be in a seeming epidemic of misery?

The answer is by no means simple. Yet I believe it is useful to look at our relationship with suffering, how that correlates with our relationship to joy, and how those relationships have been molded by technology in recent times.

There is no life without suffering. And there is no joy without sadness. Opposites inform our very existence, and it is in reconciling opposites that we actually find our peace. That being said, it is natural for us to avoid and minimize our suffering the best we know how. On the surface, it would appear that the comforts and convenience we derive from modern technology are designed to reduce our suffering. And in a way, they do. It would be crazy for most of us to 'go back in time' and start to, say, churn butter by hand or ride a horse and carriage to work or pump water to make coffee on a wood stove. However, our technological conveniences have come with hidden costs that we barely even notice.

Buddhism and Hinduism both teach that a great deal of human suffering comes from the gap between our perceptions and our desires. When we focus on the lack or absence of things we want in life, that is suffering. The manner in which technology has manifested itself in 21st century corporate-capitalist countries is to purposefully and insidiously manipulate people into feeling unfulfilled. People who are happy, content and fulfilled do not make the best consumers. And so, technology, advertising and social media are designed to shine a giant spotlight on the gap between who you are now and the hypothetical amazing life you could have if only you buy this, buy that, subscribe to this, download that.

Remember Trina and Joanne from Chapter 2? Trina made herself miserable and would not allow herself to be happy working toward her goal of being an executive at a Fortune 500 company by the age of 30. Joanne basked in joy while working just as diligently toward the same goal. Well, let's just say there are some very organized forces out there who want you to be a Trina. If you are desperately miserable with your body or your face, how much more likely are you to blindly throw all sorts of money at a company which promises to transform you into a slim, radiant, glowing supermodel with their magic elixirs? Compare that to a Joanne, who might have a loving relationship with her body even though it's not perfect (like all of our bodies), and who treats it like the divine vessel it is. If you are more like Joanne, you might feed your body healthy food, give yourself reasonable self-care and even pamper yourself without feeling the compulsion to try every cream, pill and diet the drug store has to offer.

The same can be said of any of our comforts and conveniences. A certain level of comfort is an important contributor to a happy life. Toiling endlessly to barely make ends meet is not what I believe we were put on this Earth to do. We are fortunate that we are able to benefit from the inventions of the past, to the point where a warm bed and a nutritious, balanced diet is relatively easy to obtain. But perhaps the drive to always make things more convenient, more lavish, more extreme, and more 'connected' has brought us, ironically, to a place of being more out of touch, more spoiled and perpetually unsatisfied.

Let me give you an example about convenience from my own experience. I am a busy person, and I gotta tell you, sometimes lunch for me is a bowl of instant ramen noodles and a granola bar (more often than I care to admit!). Fortunately, I like instant ramen and I appreciate the convenience that these types of foods offer me when I am in productivity mode. That being said, I would never dream of allowing that sort of highly processed food to become any kind of habit, and my heart, literally and figuratively, thanks me for it. Yesterday, I took the time to make myself a pot of homemade chili. And when I sat down to eat, I really took my time and savoured every bite in silence, being thankful for all the producers and workers who grew, processed, delivered and sold the food that I was eating. It didn't take much time out of my day, but the joy in the experience was incomparably greater than my rushed noodle bowl lunches over paperwork at my desk. In a convenience-based society, doing something that takes time and is infused with our love and attention can be incredibly meaningful. It's a form of self-care that we rarely even recognize as such, but our subconscious and our soul definitely notice it!

incredibly meaningful. It's a form of self-care that we rarely even recognize as such, but our subconscious and our soul definitely notice it!

Another thing that has changed immensely over the past 25 years in particular is how we connect with other people. To say that the Internet and social media have revolutionized communication is an understatement. Approximately 60% of the world's population has access to the Internet. Most of us in the developed world don't give a second thought to transferring many gigabytes' worth of data every day, nearly instantly. Especially lately, during the COVID-19 pandemic, more and more of our communication for work and with our friends and family is done via networked video applications. A few years back, I worked as a 'human jukebox', playing guitar and singing on cruise ships. Even while floating in the Caribbean Sea, hundreds of kilometers from any point of land, I could regularly see my daughter's face and talk to her via satellite internet (it was expensive, glitchy and slow, but I wasn't complaining!).

Again, this is wonderful technology that has enhanced our lives in many ways, and we could scarcely imagine going back to only landline telephones and 'snail mail'. But we should consider how these technologies have impacted our depth of connection with each other. Many of us are so entrenched in online communication that we all but avoid personal contact. It's no longer just young people who choose to text someone who is sitting in the next room or even across the same room. Can an 'lol' really replace the joy of laughing out loud with other people?

And beyond contact with other humans, what has our modern technological lifestyle done to our connection with other parts of nature? Multiple studies have found that anywhere from a quarter to a third of elementary school students lack basic knowledge of where foods come from (e.g. that bananas come from trees, bacon comes from pigs, and milk comes from cows, goats, and sheep.) For many people, natural environments like forests are frightening and even distasteful, rather than amazing sources of life. For decades, it seems, we have been spending less time engaged with nature and been less physically active. Fortunately, however, it may be that the tide is turning. It has been shown that Gen Z (people born after 2000) has the highest participation rate in outdoor physical activity of all the generations alive today.

I believe that avoiding the trappings of indulging in comfort and convenience while reforging an organic connection to people and to nature is quite possibly the most important building block to joy. So, given that we live in a time where we can easily become addicted to comfort and convenience, and have lost much of our connection to the vitality, life force and wisdom of the natural world, how do we as individuals, families and communities get back to a place where we can tune in and connect in more joyful ways (without going back to the Dark Ages)?

Well, let me start by getting a little spiritual philosopher on ya...

No matter whether you believe in an anthropomorphic God (aka Sky Daddy), a directive and soulful Spirit, an intelligent Universe, a Simulation or a random Universe, I think you can probably agree that there is a mysterious life force that creates order out of chaos and this crazy thing called life out of entropy. And we as living, willful beings are intimately and inextricably a part of that life force. Whether we are conscious of it or not, we are co-creating this reality with God.

Many people are uncomfortable with this notion. They want to deny their own divinity. But if you ask anyone who has had a near-death experience or a mystical experience through psychedelic drugs, or who has tried shamanic journeying, extreme fasting or meditation, they will tell you that we are all deeply connected with each other and with the great eternal Soul that is on the other side of this physical life.

The way to experience that connection is, first, by going within and loving yourself and, second, by looking outward, seeking connection and loving other living beings.

Try for a moment to remember what it was like while you were in your mother's womb. You probably had no awareness of 'self' and 'other'. There was no 'you', 'Mom' or 'Dad'. There were no neighbours Kevin and Brittany from next door or their chihuahua Bubbles. There was only a feeling of being. Your spirit was probably becoming gradually aware of your growing body, but there was no real separation of you from your environment – your mother's body provided everything you were becoming.

At that time, for all intents and purposes, you were one with the universe. And we can speculate that, at the time of your conception and prior to that moment, there was a spirit that was truly undifferentiated from the Great Spirit, and which represented the possibility of your becoming. 'You' were pure potential, pure energy waiting to manifest physically.

All of us once existed in perfect unity with the greater Universe. And we still are, on some level. Even physically, when you look at the atoms that make up our bodies, a great many of the atoms that are 'you' right now will be a part of the environment by the time you finish reading this paragraph, as you breathe out carbon dioxide that was in your blood. Conversely, many of the atoms that are in the environment will have become part of you, as the oxygen you breathe in gets incorporated into your tissues. And when we look at it in even more detail, we see that even those atoms are mostly empty space, constantly trading electrons with their neighbours. Seen at this level, it becomes rather arbitrary to set a boundary of where 'I' or 'you' end and where the 'outside' begins. You may also have noticed how we can sometimes sense another person's energy and thoughts, and even communicate in non-physical ways. All of these things make us aware that our spiritual connection goes very deep, indeed.

But despite our connections on both the physical and energetic level, our lives in these physical bodies requires us, to a certain extent, to become differentiated from our environment and to gain a unique human personality. This differentiation and individuality are a beautiful aspect of our existence here on earth, and while it would be wonderful if we could always celebrate our differences and use them to our mutual cooperative benefit, it doesn't always work that way. Our differentiated egos butt heads, land on our butts and get butt-hurt. We struggle to get our needs met and sometimes—inadvertently or deliberately—keep others from realizing their needs and wants. We develop values that are often at odds with other people's values.

Ask just about anyone who spends a good amount of time online how divided they believe the world is these days, and they might tell you that we are further apart than ever and drifting to alarming polarities. However, like the *yin* and *yang* of the Tao, the opposites we experience in this physical life can be seen as necessary codependent and dynamic forces of a greater unified whole.

The truth is that we cannot really be divided. We are all divine 'atoms' in a great cosmic soup that flows on forever.

As mentioned earlier, the way to truly experience this divine connection is initially to go inward and learn to love oneself as a divine being, and then to extend that love outward to other people and living creatures, seeing them as divine beings also.

Depending on our previous conditioning, we might find one of these more difficult than the other. Some of us might be conditioned not to think very highly of ourselves—to be overly selfless, humble or self-flagellant. Others might be conditioned to put our own interests first to an extreme level, and screw everybody else.

Speaking for myself, I initially struggled with self-love

and self-acceptance. I was conditioned to put others first, but there was a certain degree of resentfulness hiding in my altruism. I was doing a lot of things for others, but it wasn't coming from a great place, because I didn't truly love myself. Through much of my depression, I wanted to do great things for humanity but I didn't feel worthy. I had grand dreams but I wouldn't accept help or even reach out to do small kindnesses because I was scared of what people thought of me.

After I did some spiritual work in the form of reading, meditation and speaking to wise folk, I came to a realization that I was connected to the Divine and an imperfect, living part of it. I became less concerned about appearances, and I finally allowed myself to shine brighter. Of course, I'm not perfect and never will be, but I come to my interactions with others from a much more loving place now that I have a better relationship with myself. When I am conscious of our intrinsic energetic connection, I am more likely to make more meaningful interpersonal connections. I see other people as spirits trying to navigate this physical world, and that helps me to treat people with more empathy and to want to cooperate as much as possible.

It can also be very challenging—downright difficult sometimes—to see others as divine beings too, especially when they are acting like assholes! But we all forget our connection - it's part of our humanity to be constantly forgetting and reminding ourselves, and that's why we act like assholes. It's by loving each other in our imperfection that we become connected with our divinity.

Now, getting back to our high-convenience, tech-connected culture...

One thing that is exciting about our world is that, even though we are often fragmented, isolated and environmentally threatened by technology, there are many meaningful and enlightening connections happening through the Internet. I see great work being done by millions of spiritually- and community-minded folks and organizations around the world. Today's young people, especially, seem to me to be increasingly self-aware, globally-focused and lovingly supportive of their peers. And these good vibrations are being amplified and spread by technology. We have a lot to struggle against: the widening gap between rich and poor, environmental destruction, systemic racism, overpopulation and violence of all sorts. However, there are great forces of spiritual warriors who are making better, faster, more meaningful and more powerful connections every day, and as such, spreading joy despite the circumstances. For that, I am very grateful...which brings us to our next chapter...

chapter 6

The Big G – Gratitude

OK, so up to this point, we've explored a few challenging but, I think, attainable steps toward a more joyful life—namely, embracing your journey, avoiding the 'happily-ever-after' pitfalls, making that all-important *choice* to live joyfully, focusing mainly on the present and the future, and seeking out meaningful connections to other people and to nature. But now, we are really going to kick things up a notch by taking a close look at gratitude.

Now, gratitude has been an extremely hot topic in the fields of positive psychology, high performance coaching, manifestation theory and overall mental wellness over the past few decades. And I believe it is for good reason. An 'attitude of gratitude' is probably one of the most important, if not the most important, things you can do to set yourself up for happiness.

You may be saying to yourself that you already are very grateful, and no doubt you already are. I always felt that I had an attitude of gratitude, for the most part. However, I found that once I made gratitude a habit rather than just feeling it whenever it popped up, I really started to 'raise my vibe' and set myself up for more joy.

The most effective habit for me personally was to train myself to think about things I am grateful for immediately upon waking and just before going to sleep. I'd have to say this is the most powerful happiness hack that I have ever used, so if you were to implement only one regular practise from this book, this may be the best.

How you practise this is completely up to you, however. Some people find, especially in the beginning, that it is helpful to write your blessings down in a journal. I did this for a while to lock in the habit, but once I got into the swing of things, I began to simply review in my mind a few things that I am grateful for—once before falling asleep, and again before I got out of bed in the morning.

The first few moments and the last few moments of waking consciousness are very powerful. When you first wake up, you are typically in an alpha brainwave state. The alpha state is considered the gateway to the subconscious mind. So if you are able to train yourself to get into a positive frame of mind as soon as possible upon waking, you are sending signals to your subconscious that are positive, and you are more likely to carry a positive attitude throughout your day. (Additionally, some of the other things you can do within the first half hour of being awake are to recite or listen to affirmations, to visualize productive outcomes for your day or your future, or to recite your personal mission statement to yourself. It's generally best to start by focusing on gratitude for some time, and then adding these other practises gradually, if and when you feel ready for them.)

Focusing on gratitude twice a day in this way can not only make you feel more joyful, but it can also put you in a mental and energetic state where you are more prepared to receive more good things in your life. People who believe in the law of attraction assert that being grateful is a key to attracting abundance and positive outcomes. And I must admit that when I first started my gratitude practise, my intent had a lot to do with attracting more wealth and success. But for me, the greater benefit of gratitude is how it has shifted my mind frame to one that is so much more joyful and full of life. By focusing on what we are grateful for, we begin to realize how many blessings we have, and our perception of our reality becomes more positive. As Dr. Wayne Dyer famously said, 'If you change the way you look at things, the things you look at change'.

Feeling and expressing gratitude gives a tremendous boost to our choice to be joyful, and it helps us to overcome 'happily-ever-after' syndrome, because it fuels our joy even when it seems we are far from attaining our goals and our circumstances aren't the greatest. We may not be exactly where we want to be, but look at all the wonderful things we can be thankful for! Even the simplest things can be part of that list and help to put us in a grateful and receptive state of mind: we can be thankful for our warm blankets, our shoes, fresh fruit, our muscles, a candle-lit bath, a cuddle session with our pet.

You might be thinking, 'I'm in a horrible situation. Why should I be thankful?' If that's the case, it may be true that you have fewer blessings to be thankful for, and it can be very easy to fall into a mindset of feeling sorry for yourself or being angry at the world for your misfortune. I wouldn't blame you for having those feelings, and I would encourage you to honour them and give them their proper place, but it is important not to get trapped in those feelings and get overwhelmed by the suffering of them to the point where they consume you.

Rather, acknowledge that your situation is bad, but take the time to find even the smallest things to be grateful for. Begin with your breath. All of our life, our connection, our spiritual being begins with breath. Be thankful for your breath and then move on to the next simplest things you can be thankful for. Your eyes, your ears, your fingers your toes. Do you have a warm place to sleep? Be thankful for that. Do you have anyone who is kind to you? Be grateful for them.

Also, have faith that whatever your situation, it will get better, and be thankful for that. Take even just a few minutes a day to imagine yourself in a better place, and be grateful for that in advance. Not only will this train your mind to expect better things and help to put you into a more joyful state, but it is also one of the key aspects of manifestation theory, which is the bringing forth of things you want via thoughts, beliefs, emotions and action.

While it is not the aim of this book to get in a detailed discussion of manifestation (there are many great books that
delve deeply into that subject), I will share with you a personal example of how gratitude played a part in manifesting
a fabulous experience in my life.

In 2015, I was working two day jobs, a full-time job as a
call centre technical support person for a cellular network
provider, and a part-time job at a liquor store, while also pur-
suing my passion-career as a performing singer-songwriter.
As you can imagine, my day jobs did not afford me a lot of
time to write, rehearse and play shows, but I did the best I
could. I had a girlfriend at the time who had just started a
new job managing a coffeeshop, and I visited her there a few
days in. The guy she was replacing was also a musician, a
bass player who had worked on cruise ships. When we met,
he asked me what kind of cover song repertoire I had. Even
though I was currently playing mostly original material, I had
played in cover bands for many years and had an extensive
repertoire. He told me that he still played cruise ships from
time to time, that he had some contacts in the industry and
that I should consider applying.

While I had considered applying to land-based tropical
resorts in the past, I hadn't given it much serious thought.
But now, this possibility of playing on the high seas and
visiting tropical islands for a living was really sparking
my imagination!

I had been working with manifestation and gratitude
practises for a few years, and had made some progress from a
difficult post-divorce, under-employed situation to one that

was looking significantly better, but this gave me a manifestation goal to really sink my teeth into. I started by creating a vision board with all sorts of photos of cruise ships, beaches and tropical cityscapes, surrounded by words of gratitude: 'I am so happy and grateful for my exciting and lucrative cruise ship soloist job!'

Each night before bed and any other time I thought about it, I would visualize myself performing for happy vacationers on a huge ship. Meanwhile, I worked diligently on resurrecting and beefing up my repertoire of popular songs (because you need to put in the work too!).

Finally, when I contacted the entertainment director at the cruise line head office, I made sure I was feeling supremely confident that I would get the job. While we had a good first discussion, the big hurdle was still to come—I had to submit an online audition and interview. I put up a black curtain in my bedroom and recorded a dozen or so songs, again imagining myself playing them on a sunny Caribbean cruise. I recorded my interview and excitedly submitted the package. There was nothing left to do but wait...and be thankful for the job I believed with all my heart I would get.

And yes, several weeks later I was accepted and got my first assignment, which would have been sailing out of Baltimore for Caribbean destinations. I say 'would have' because about a month before I was to set sail, I had a freak accident which severed the tendon in the middle finger of my left hand. The injury, known as mallet finger, was going to take eight weeks or more to heal! I was, of course, devastated, but I wasn't going to let that stop me. I continued to stay grateful as I contacted the entertainment director to inform him of my plight. I waited with bated breath for several days for his reply. Fortunately, they were able to re-assign me to a new ship shortly after my scheduled recovery. Now I just had to focus on my physiotherapy and on finishing things up at my two jobs.

Let me tell you, I have never been happier to resign from two jobs in my life. A few months later, I set sail into an amazing adventure which covered three contracts, a year-and-a-half, dozens of exciting sunny destinations, playing for thousands of people and making lots of new friends from around the world!

Now, did an attitude of gratitude do all the work for me? Of course not. I had to network, practise, fill out paperwork, do my finger strength and flexibility exercises, and learn the words to dozens of classic rock songs. But I really don't know if I would have made that dream a reality if I wasn't practising gratitude on the daily. In fact, as much as it sounds like a 'happily-ever-after' story, I was actually very grateful for the tech support and liquor store jobs I had before this opportunity came my way. I believe that was part of the magic formula as well.

Again, once you start practising it regularly, you will likely find that the greatest benefit of daily gratitude is the shift in your consciousness to more positivity and more joy. And you don't have to take my word for it. Over the past few decades, science has taken in interest in how gratitude can impact our health, happiness and well-being. In their 'white paper' which cites over 200 academic articles, UC Berkeley's Greater Good Science Center concludes the following:

> Research suggests that gratitude may be associated with many benefits for individuals, including better physical and psychological health, increased happiness and life satisfaction, decreased materialism, and more.
>
> A handful of studies suggest that more grateful people may be healthier, and others suggest that scientifically designed practises to increase gratitude can also improve people's health and encourage them to adopt healthier habits.
>
> Many more studies have examined possible connections between gratitude and various elements of psychological well-being. In general, more grateful people are happier, more satisfied with their lives, less materialistic, and less likely to suffer from burnout. (Allen, 2018)

While the physiological correlates of gratitude are many, the main benefit of gratitude is that it increases the production of dopamine and serotonin in the brain. These are our two main 'feel good' neurotransmitters, which influence pleasure, reward, motivation and mood. So when you are grateful, you are giving yourself a natural high as well as contributing to your overall wellbeing. Sounds like joy to me!

I also feel that, from the point of view of both creating joy and manifesting our goals, it is important for gratitude to become ingrained, beyond even a habit. Ideally, it should become second nature to us. In order to truly make our lives better, it is best if we are operating from a mindset of gratitude as a matter of course. When we get to that point, both our conscious mind and our subconscious are working at a more grateful and thus joyful level. A potential added bonus is that manifestation theory experts suggest that much of the power in our ability to manifest comes from our subconscious mind.

Think about it this way: if you are deeply grateful for the things you want, as if you already have them, and that feeling of gratitude is ingrained in your deepest levels, you will start to carry yourself with a confidence and an alignment that will tend to bring those things closer to you. This is what manifestation theory calls being 'on the same frequency' as the thing you want. And as you can probably imagine, being on the same frequency as what you want is a pretty joyful experience.

So, what are some steps you can take to ingrain an attitude of gratitude in your day-to-day life?

As with most practises, you will eventually need to find what works best for you. As for me, I began by writing down my blessings every day. This practise came from an exercise in Rhonda Byrne's *The Magic,* to write down ten things you are grateful for every day for at least 28 days. Once I had done that, I continued to journal occasionally, but I began to 'think my blessings' for a few minutes each day immediately upon waking and just before going to bed.

My morning gratitude is usually focused on my current situation and the day ahead. It goes something like this:

> 'Thank you, thank you, thank you for another glorious day! I am so grateful for my health, my strong muscles, my keen senses and my healthy organs. I am thankful for the roof over my head, the food I am going to eat today and the money that I have to buy the things that I need. Thank you for my friends, my family and my pets. This is going to be such an amazing day, and I am grateful to be of service and for the work that I will accomplish today.'

(Just for the record, I also recite my personal mission statement out loud to myself in the mirror: *'My mission is to assist and encourage others in finding and maintaining a sustainable sense of joy, calm and healing, through workshops, writing and speaking.'* And I have one other little pep talk that I say in my head before I start my day: *'Winner attitude, winner habits, winner results.'*)

I try to start my morning gratitude the moment I realize that I am awake. I can't say I have a 100% track record with that, but I can safely say that before my feet hit the floor, I've had several grateful thoughts, and it greatly increases the chances that I begin my day with an effective and positive mindset.

My evening gratitude is a little bit different: it is more focused on things that actually happened that day. When I lie down in bed, I do **a** little review of my day and choose a half-dozen or so events, situations, people or things I was grateful for that day. For example, *'Thank you for the great day I had with my daughter. I am grateful for the great song-writing session. I am so thankful for the great meal my friend made for me.'*

Other times, I might choose to do a 'manifesting' gratitude session, which is being thankful in advance for things or situations I would like to have in the future. This is one of the ways we can put ourselves in tune with the 'vibration' of having something. With this type of work, it is important to think of the situation as already being fulfilled, rather than something that is in process. Otherwise, your subconscious may view it as always being on the way or out of reach.

With these three types of gratitude practise, I have gotten accustomed to being thankful for my past, ongoing and future blessings. One benefit of this type of 'structured' gratitude is that it primes your mind to be more aware of grateful emotions that spontaneously arise throughout the day. As this happens consistently, with more and more frequency, you are well on your way to living a more joyful existence.

chapter 7

Purpose and Contribution

One of my biggest struggles through most of my adult life has been my work and career. When I was young, I was conditioned to please the adults in my life, and the majority of those adults invariably steered me toward a 'sensible' career. I was a multi-talented kid, and I was curious about a lot of things, so I convinced myself that it made sense to examine my range of interests and focus on the ones that would have a better income potential. And so, my early career path was a straightforward combination of exercise physiology, the scientific method and teaching. And looking back, that could have been a great purpose, one that I could have been proud of. But there was something powerful telling me that wasn't my true purpose. At the time, I didn't have the emotional, mental and spiritual maturity to reflect, process and understand that gap between my 'doing' and my 'being'. I just knew that I was desperately unhappy in my job,

I was self-medicating in unhealthy ways and I didn't have the resourcefulness or the courage to turn it around.

I felt there was a purpose out there somewhere for me, a *destiny* even, but I didn't know what that was. I was completely lost, floating, feeling like an underachiever and a loser. I was mired in procrastination and self-loathing. I was failing at a job I didn't even want, and even though I was finding some solace in writing songs, I felt like I wasn't good enough at that to make a livelihood out of it (and honestly, at that time I probably wasn't).

When I finally quit my job as a university instructor, I was 32 years old, struggling with drinking, gambling and depression. I needed a reset. I did what many people did at a much younger age: I went backpacking in Europe. I spent a few weeks in Holland and a few in Spain, visiting museums, writing in coffeeshops, hiking, busking and dancing with the younger backpackers in the discos at night. It held all of the artsy, historical romance that I expected. And most importantly, it gave me some time and space to get to know myself better, and to 'find myself' as they say.

In a fairy tale version of this story, I might have had a great epiphany, found my calling and returned to Canada to embark on my new mission. The real-life version is a little messier. I did draw a ton of inspiration from my month abroad. It sowed the seed for what my mission would become years later. At the most basic level, I realized that even though objectivity is important, I could not limit myself to scientifically breaking down the world into small, manageable pieces. I knew that I was here to explore the subjective side of the human experience, to apply my learning to the art of songwriting and to 'live my life as a work of art'. Yet, there was also a nebulous hint that I was somehow to become a 'healer'. This call was quite strong in my soul, but I had no idea how it would take shape.

While I believe my own personal healing began with that trip, it would be over a decade before I would get clarity around my life's purpose. And the frustration of knowing it was there but not being able to figure it out caused tremendous inner turmoil, even though I was (mostly) holding it together on the outside.

For the next decade, I worked odd jobs – packaging coffee, teaching at a private school, working as a farmhand – and was also a stay-at-home dad to my daughter, while trying to do as much music as I could. Even though all those things were meaningful and should have provided me a sense of purpose, I wasn't satisfied. I walked through life with a gnawing sense that I was supposed to 'be something more'.

If my current self could visit that old me, I would probably tell him to embrace the joy and purpose of those roles, to live them as fully and joyfully as possible, and to have faith that my higher purpose would become apparent as I lived purposefully in the now. But instead of acknowledging my innate divinity and accepting that I was enough in that moment, I suffered because all I saw was my lack. It was a 'saviour complex,' where my ego wanted to save the world, but I wasn't even doing great things in my own little world because I was miserable that I wasn't *more*.

Now, in my case I was consciously desperate for a

greater purpose, but I believe there are also people who are depressed mainly because they lack *any* sense of purpose. They live an aimless life, chasing pleasures that have very little meaning. They are on auto-pilot. Maybe they have low self-esteem. Perhaps they are working jobs they hate in order to buy material possessions and party on the weekends. They may be unaware that they can even have a purpose, thinking that is only for the 'special' among us. Or indeed, they are so jaded with our society's systems that they want nothing to do with having a purpose. You might say they are in survival mode, which is simply hanging on for dear life, and is a difficult position for anyone to experience any sort of growth.

From a spiritual standpoint, many people believe that we are born into our circumstances in order to learn or accomplish certain things, or that Spirit/God/the Universe has an intended purpose for us, and it is our 'job' to realize what our soul's purpose is. Whether or not you have that sort of spiritual belief does not really matter, as I think we can have a meaningful life without believing in a higher power. The key, I think, is simpler: that we all have an inner desire to spend a significant portion of our time doing things that are important and meaningful to us. (And hey, let's throw 'fun' in there, too, because fun can give us clues as to what our purpose is.)

Figuring out what is important, meaningful and fun to you is the critical first step to having purpose. The other part is figuring out where your values and talents fit in the world. As Frederick Buechner put it, 'Vocation is the place where our deep gladness meets the world's deep need.'

Look at that term: 'deep gladness'. Sounds like joy, doesn't it? So, not only does having purpose contribute to our ability to experience joy, but likewise, the things that bring us the most joy can be a spotlight that informs us of our purpose. This sense of purpose does not necessarily have to come from our career or paid work. For many of us, our most meaningful activities come from other arenas in our lives: parenting, volunteering, romantic partnerships, hobbies and friendships can all contribute to our sense of purpose.

Below I have mapped out five levels of purposeful living that I believe correlate very strongly to one's mental and emotional wellness. Don't worry if you feel like you are currently at level 1 or 2 – I think is probably the norm, because this is not something that is stressed in popular culture.

Levels of Purposeful Living

1. Not even aware that you have a life's purpose (autopilot).
2. Feel that you have, might have or 'should' have a purpose, but don't know what it is.
3. Know your purpose, but don't know how to live it.
4. Know your purpose and are living it, but are consistently overwhelmed by it.
5. Know your purpose and are living it in a healthy, fulfilling and joyful way.

I feel strongly that people who work at getting to #5 are going to tend to have a more joyful life, and greater mental and emotional well-being, in the long run. That's not to say that there aren't people out there living joyfully on autopilot, but I think just being guided by the principle of your purpose can go a long way to creating a more joyful life.

As you may have guessed from reading my personal story, I was at #2 and #3 for most of my adult life. For me, it wasn't that I didn't know my purpose, but that I was very reluctant to choose a path and commit to it. I was so busy trying to define my perfect life that I wasn't getting out and living it. So, even though a sense of purpose and meaning is important, it is also important not to get blocked by a quixotic quest for your ultimate purpose. Instead, search for meaning and purpose *where you are now* and live that. If some missing piece is still nagging you, that's OK. You can fill it in later.

Let's face it, probably only a tiny fraction of the population actually grasp their sense of purpose fully right off the bat and get down to the business of living it. Most of us don't, and that's OK. We have a more complicated set of societal role structures than ever before. Your purpose is bound to be a little complicated. While there have been many great books on discovering your purpose (such as *The Gifts of Imperfection* by Brené Brown), let's take a look at how you might quickly get a better feel for the important and meaningful things that contribute to your sense of purpose and joy.

Looking Inward and Embracing Your Uniqueness

Before we look at some specific questions you can ask yourself to help you get a clearer sense of purpose, let's just take a moment to realize that everyone's journey is unique, and that the route you take to find your purpose (and ultimately your joy) is going to be different from anyone else's. And, there is much to be said for simply ***asking***!

I am a big fan of concepts such as 'our higher self' and 'spirit guides'. In the end, there may not actually be anyone 'out there,' but I think, even if those concepts are simply a place marker for your own subconscious mind, the larger YOU knows the answer to many things that you currently feel clueless about, and the act of asking questions directly can often bring answers to the surface.

Asking your higher self for guidance can be as simple as getting yourself into a quiet, meditative state and then asking the question and seeing what comes to your mind. However, some people find it helpful to use a visualization technique such as this:

Sit or lie down in a comfortable position for you, close your eyes and inhale deeply through the nostrils. When you exhale, constrict your throat slightly and make a breathy 'Ha' sound. As you continue to breathe in this way, count down from 10 to 1, feeling yourself become more and more relaxed on each exhalation. When you reach 1, resume breathing normally.

Tense up the muscles in your feet by curling your toes for 5-10 seconds. As you relax them, focus on how light they now feel, almost as if they are floating. Now contract your calf muscles by pointing your toes for 5-10 seconds, relax and feel the lightness and floating sensation in your lower legs.

Continue going up your body, flexing, relaxing and

floating each muscle group – thighs, stomach, chest, arms, hands, neck and finally your facial muscles. By the time you have reached your face, your whole body now feels light, as if you are floating. Take a moment to enjoy this sensation.

Next, imagine a movie screen. On the movie screen is a beautiful forest scene with an elevator that appears to go up into the clouds.

Use the floating sensation in your body to imagine yourself floating up off the ground and gently toward the screen. When you reach the screen, you are surprised that it is not solid, and you pass right through it and into the forest scene. Take a moment to notice the sights, smells and sensations.

Now press the 'up' button on the elevator, and when the doors open step in. A smiling woman is there with you – her relaxing presence is putting you at ease as you ascend into the clouds. When you reach the top, you step out into the clouds to see two couches. In one of them is your Higher Self, who invites you to sit on the other couch, and asks you how they can help.

Respectfully ask your Higher Self to tell you about your life's purpose and wait for them to respond. Continue the conversation for as long as you need.

When you are satisfied, give thanks to your Higher Self and intend that you will remember everything about the conversation. Get back into the elevator and come down. Float back into your body and take very deep breaths, returning to a refreshed state of consciousness.

This visualization really gets your right brain involved in the process of exploring your purpose. As such, the answers you get might be a little bit fuzzy or even puzzling. That's OK – just make a note of the impressions that you get and trust that your mind will make sense of them. Or, you might be more of a left brain thinker, and the whole exercise really didn't work for you. That's OK, too. You might benefit more by simply brainstorming in a more traditional way regarding your life's purpose. In any case, asking yourself some tangible questions about meaning and purpose can help to clarify your thinking. The following are a few questions you might consider:

What gets you into the flow state?

Or, as author Mark Manson says, 'What makes you forget to eat and poop?'

You might have heard the term 'flow', meaning a highly-focused state of mind where you are effortlessly absorbed in an activity, often performing at your best and losing track of time. We also call this being 'in the zone', and when it happens the rest of the world tends to fall away and you can literally forget to have lunch. (We are going dig deeper into flow in Chapter 10.)

What are the types of tasks that can get you into the flow state? These activities can hold clues about or even point directly to your life's purpose.

When I first started university, before moving on to exercise science, I studied computer science. In coding, the basic workflow is to design your algorithm, write your code and then debug it. I was at best a mediocre algorithm designer and a pretty good code writer, but I was a star debugger. Getting code to work properly got me into a flow state. In those days, we worked on banks of mainframe terminals in a computer lab (yes, I'm *that* old), so several students would be in the lab working at once on an assignment. Now, in those days I was also a master procrastinator and a bit of a moocher. I would often stroll into the lab with a few hours left before the deadline and pester one of my classmates (who had worked on the assignment all week but was struggling to debug their code) to have a look at their program because I had not done the algorithm groundwork. Then, as I was writing my code, I would quickly slip into the zone, bang it out in record time and then get down to debugging, where I would breeze through and usually finish before my classmates, much to their chagrin and frustration. Fortunately, I'm not that much of a jerk, and I would usually return the favour and help them debug their code. Usually.

Surprising as it may seem, the flow of debugging code is very similar to the flow of writing lyrics (at least for me). Solving problems using the syntax of a computer language and building a song within a poetic structure using the syntax of the English language and the language of music are both things that got me into flow. Whether I realized it or not, these were clues that my purpose might include creating meaning and structure out of words and sounds.

So, take a look at what gets you into the flow and makes you forget to eat. Playing with children? Organizing a party?

Cooking an elaborate meal? Rebuilding an engine? Again, don't get caught in the trap of thinking it necessarily has to be something you can or want to make a living at. Even if it doesn't directly translate to a career, it may still hold clues to your purpose and what is important to you.

What gets you fired up (or pissed off)?

What is it that gets you really excited, either in a positive way or angrier than a bull in a rodeo chute? The things we are passionate about can often become our purpose. Exploring what really gets your fire going can give clues to what your life's purpose might be. For me, the things that excite me inform my purpose pretty closely. Nothing compares to the feeling of finishing a song, or putting on a great performance, or helping someone overcome a hurdle to their more joyful life. Those things really help to define my purpose as an artist and a healer.

This may seem like a no-brainer, however, not every passion is going to be a purpose, and your purpose might not be immediately obvious from your passions. For example, you might be passionate about the outdoors and the environment. You might get really fired up about spending your weekends in a cabin in the woods and volunteering with an environmental advocacy organization, but perhaps helping other people learn about finances holds greater importance and sense of purpose for you.

Your purpose may also be related to your passions, but not blatantly obvious. I have a friend who is very creative, went to art school, did design work for a while and made jewelry. Despite having great passion in those areas, it turned out she found a sense of purpose in running a lovingly-curated crystal and metaphysical shop with a welcoming and healing atmosphere. Her eye for beautiful things and a desire to inspire, encourage and empower people became a calling that was aligned with but slightly removed from the things that fired her up.

What gets you curious?

Some people are driven by curiosity. It's not so much about what they want to do, it's about what they want to learn. What gets you lost in reading, exploring, wandering or diving down a rabbit-hole of documentaries?

For many years, I was intensely curious about altered states of conscious, spiritual 'enlightenment', esoteric healing modalities and the possible effects of faith on physical health and healing. I wasn't studying it for any concrete purpose, and it wasn't until years later that it had any real impact on my sense of purpose. I just knew it was fascinating and fun to read about.

Many of us consider learning as a means to various ends, while others value learning for its own sake and find their purpose in furthering humanity's understanding of a field of knowledge. Whether your curiosity leads you to apply knowledge to worthwhile activities or takes you on a quest of research and learning, exploring what piques your curiosity can help you to hone in on your sense of purpose.

How do you feel inspired to serve?

I would say that purpose is most often related to service in some way. Our most important activities are often those which benefit others, and we feel better when we are helping others or the world. However, when many people think of service, they think of it as a chore, or a less-than-pleasant responsibility or obligation. This point of view shifts when we realize service can bring us a sense of camaraderie, accomplishment, pride and joy. I think the shift in perspective is beautifully summed up in this poem by Rabindranath Tagore:

> *I slept and dreamt that life was joy.*
> *I awoke and saw that life was service.*
> *I acted and behold, service was joy.*

In the first part of our lives, we often see joy as the pursuit of pleasure or happiness. Then, we are often rudely awoken into a workforce that sees us as cogs in the machine, so that many of us come to know service as thankless drudgery. But if we are fortunate, we can grow to see that service can bring us tremendous happiness. It has been shown repeatedly in experiments that doing things for others makes us happier than doing things for our own benefit.

The beneficiaries of our service can be targeted individuals, groups or the general population. Many of us feel called to serve people who are suffering from afflictions or circumstances similar to the ones that we ourselves have suffered. We have a natural empathy for those who have similar challenges, and our experience often gives us tools to help in an understanding way.

The passions we examined in the previous section can also give us direction as to how and who we might serve. If, for example, you are passionate about learning and get fired up about children's mental and emotional well-being, you might be called to serve as a school guidance counsellor. Or if you are passionate about music and fairness, you might want to serve musicians by working for a performance rights organization that helps them get paid for the use of their music.

Serving others has become a tremendous source of joy for me. When I feel that I have helped someone to overcome an emotional roadblock or made them feel more relaxed and vibrant, I am on top of the world. I like to think that when this happens, I have in a small way made an impact in a person's life, and maybe even made the world a little bit better place. It is an immensely joyful feeling.

Again, everyone's journey toward a sense of purpose is going to be different. Listening to your inner voice and exploring what gets you into the flow, what gets you fired up, what makes you curious and how you wish to serve will give you a great framework for discovering your unique purpose. From there, aligning yourself with that purpose and taking actions that you feel good about will contribute greatly to your self-worth, your fulfillment and ultimately your joy!

chapter 8

Work and Money

Money can't buy you happiness,
but it helps you look for it in a lot more places.

- Milton Berle

I grew up not far from the city of Moncton, New Brunswick. Situated near the geographic center of Canada's Maritime provinces, Moncton is known as the Hub City, and was historically a transportation and logistical hub in the region. The bilingual town continues to be a bustling center, with thriving transportation, communication, information technology and retail sectors. It also has always been known for its vibrant nightlife. With a large population of fairly affluent young professionals supporting the high-tech industries and looking to blow off steam and their hard-earned paycheques, Moncton has long been known as a 'work hard, play hard' kind of city. Of course not everyone lives that way, but there is palpable vibe to the city that says 'we go to work primarily to make money, so that we can do more things in our spare time that bring us joy.'

My current home is a few hours' drive away, in the Annapolis Valley of Nova Scotia. Historically, 'the Valley,' as locals call it, has been an agricultural stronghold known in particular for its apples, although in recent years many orchards have been converted to vineyards to supply a burgeoning wine industry. The Valley's beautiful natural environment and hospitality have also been fertile ground for a booming tourism sector. In the hippie era of the 1970s, an influx of US draft-dodgers and a community of Shambala Buddhists who relocated from Colorado brought a colourful mix to the traditional rural communities here—a cultural flavouring that seems to have persisted to this day, leading to an entrepreneurial class that I playfully refer to as 'business hippies.' Traditional farmers have had to become more entrepreneurial as well, turning to value-added strategies to combat the competition of cheap produce being shipped in from other countries. As a result, the Valley has a very artisanal feel, where the small creative business is king. Again, not everyone is this way, but the overall vibe here says, 'we work primarily as an expression of our values and creativity, and so we derive a good portion of our joy from our work.'

Having lived both a 'work hard, play hard' and a conscious entrepreneurial lifestyle, I can safely say that neither one is inherently superior to the other. It is a matter of personal choice, and you may also find yourself moving from one mode to another as your career progresses. It is a privilege if you are in a position to make this sort of choice.

That being said, there is a disheartening trend in many parts of the world, where it is practically a given that the majority of people will be resigned to working jobs that they hate in order to pursue a type of happiness that is fleeting at best and, at worst, superficial, unfulfilling and fake. Working hard so that you can play hard is a totally legitimate ethos to follow, but what if your hard work becomes soul-killing and your hard play is just chasing the next meaningless high in a vain attempt to soothe your dying soul?

Yikes.

It sounds dramatic and desperate, but unfortunately it is a reality for many, many people. How can we avoid this trap, or if we already find ourselves there, escape it? How do we face the necessity of having a livelihood and making money without sacrificing joy?

It might be helpful to start by going back to basics and examining our views of money. Our beliefs, attitudes and feelings around money can be tremendously complicated. But if we strip it down to its simplest definition, money is just a universally agreed-upon system of exchange. Its main advantage over a barter system is that you don't have to find someone with a matching exchange proposition for it to work. Say you have a diamond ring and you want to trade it for a guitar. In a barter system, you would have to find someone with a guitar who wants a diamond ring. And, you both have to agree that the trade is fair, otherwise one of you might have to sweeten the deal by throwing in a chicken and a roll of duct tape. See, money is a real time and effort saver!

Now, of course, you're probably thinking that it is way more complicated than that, and it is. However, this simple example is a good starting point for breaking down our fears and hang-ups around money. Perhaps you were told as a child that money was the root of all evil, or your parents resented their jobs, or complained constantly that there was never enough, or that rich people got that way by being unscrupulous. To be able to find joy in making and spending money, you will need to rewrite those negative scripts you may have carried with you thus far.

Jen Sincero's book *You Are a Badass At Making Money* provides some great tools and exercises for making this shift in thinking. But for our purposes here, let's start with a few simple exercises to get more joyful about money.

First, physically write out on a piece of paper two or three negative beliefs you were conditioned to hold about money. For example,

1. Having a lot of money leads to corruption.
2. Rich people are usually greedy and mean.
3. I need to be cut-throat to make a lot of money.

Even though you may have held onto these ideas for decades, I'm sure you can appreciate how they might be holding you back from making all the money you deserve. So now, try a little exercise called 'Return to Sender'. Realize that these limiting (and untrue!) beliefs came from other people – parents, teachers or friends. And for each one, say to yourself (out loud is best), 'I return this belief to sender, with love and light attached' and feel it healed within yourself. If you want, you can burn the paper to give you visual confirmation and a sense of finality.

Second, decide on what beliefs will take the place of the old ones. For example,

1. Having lots of money would allow me to help the people I love.
2. Rich people are no different than poor people, they just have better resources.
3. I can joyfully make a lot of money doing things I love.

Whatever new beliefs you decide on, memorize them, repeat them several times a day, and really try to feel their truth deep inside you.

Third, get in the habit of being grateful for the money you have earned and have been given in the past, the money that you have now and the money that will come to you in the future. Remember gratitude? The Big G? It is very helpful in feeling more joy around money. One particularly power-ful practise is to be thankful for the services for which you receive bills. When you get your power bill, instead of griping about having to pay it, be thankful for the electricity you used to heat your bath water, light your home and cook your food.

If you have deep, stubborn issues around money that are impacting your ability to live more joyfully, I would suggest that you invest some time in working those out, either by reading Ms. Sincero's book (or if you want a deeper dive, *Money: Master the Game* by Tony Robbins), or by actually hiring a counselor, financial advisor or coach to help you work through those issues and adopt a healthier financial mindset. For most people, however, I believe that if you work on replacing negative beliefs and maintaining a mindset of gratitude, you can heal your relationship with money to the point where you can use it to accentuate your joy, rather than having it be an albatross around your neck.

Now, what about the relationship between work, money and joy?

As we explored in the example of the two communities described at the beginning of this chapter, some people will find a lot of inherent joy in the work they do. These are often the people that combine their passion and purpose into their work life. Other people may simply have a job to pay the bills, and derive most of their joy from their leisure time. And there's nothing wrong with either of those approaches.

As a musician, I know many people who, when they tried to make a livelihood out of playing music, lost a lot of the joy they felt from making music in the first place. And so, going back to having a day job that paid well enough to finance their serious musical hobby was a tremendous success for them. If you work 9 to 5 as a financial planner and it's just alright – it's not killing your soul – and you find incredible joy in live action role playing games on the weekends, what's wrong with that? Or, if you live and breathe the work you do as an interior designer, to the degree that it fuels you and you don't need to follow other interests or take long vacations to rejuvenate yourself, more power to you!

Regardless of our approach, both work and money can be

sources of joy and of pain. Having money to spare can take a lot of the stress out of our lives and also give us opportunities to explore our world in different ways that can bring us more joy (as expressed in the Milton Berle quote at the beginning of this chapter). The work we do for a living, in its capacity to inspire, to help others, to provide basic needs to our society and to express our creativity, can be very joyful in and of itself.

But if you are in a position where you are not getting a lot of joy out of your work, nor are you being well compensated for your work, how can you turn this around so that you are drawing more joy out of your work-money situation?

As mentioned earlier, money is a system of enumerating the value of products and services. When we do work, whether for others or as self-employment, the ideal is that we are paid money in accordance to the value we provide to an employer, our customers or the world at large. The more value you provide, the more you are paid, in an ideal world. There are discrepancies and injustices that occur – many people are not paid what they are worth, while many others seem to have way more money coming in than they could ever need despite not providing a great deal of value. However, over time and over a vast ocean of transactions, the market does tend to reward people and companies that provide the greatest value.

So, whether you feel you are in the right job or not, one of the best ways to set yourself up for future success is to examine what level of value you are providing at the moment and try to come up with ways that you can provide more value to the world. Can you further educate yourself or add a new skill? Can you create a product that many people will find useful or valuable in their lives? Can you assist others to make their lives or jobs easier? Can you find a more efficient way of doing things than your company is currently using? Can you teach people a skill that you have?

If you feel that you are almost ready to leave your current position, these types of questions may help you to figure out where you are headed and how you might make a living in a more joyful way. If you are not ready to make a move just yet, questions such as these can help to make you more valuable in your current work place, hopefully leading to some more money, a sense of ownership in your job, more confidence and hopefully more joy.

At the end of the day, we typically spend nearly a third of our lives doing work. Do we really want to be miserable during all that time? We can easily end up feeling trapped by our work. After all, we need to eat, clothe our children, heat our homes. However, there are often many more opportunities available than we think when we feel stuck. Often, all we need is to shift our mindset from one of feeling trapped and hopeless to one of feeling grateful for our current and future opportunities

Being grateful for your current job as a mail room clerk, doing it with a smile and being the absolute best mail room clerk anyone could imagine will set you up with the mindset you need to get the hell out of that mail room and into a job that is more worthy of your joy! Moping around hating your jobs doesn't get you anywhere. Be grateful, do your current job well and have faith that the right match for you will come your way.

A quick note here as well about what we call work-life balance: we can all use more of it. For people who see their job as simply a means to other ends that are more joyful, this is a no-brainer. Balancing 'work' and 'life' can be a tremendous challenge, but when there is clear separation between the two, it is simply a matter of not being overwhelmed by your job and its responsibilities, and being able to devote as much time and energy to yourself and your family, friends and hobbies as possible.

For those whose work is very much a source of their joy and identity, work-life balance is still important, but the lines are usually fuzzier. I'm one of those people who has striven to find and create work that is meaningful to me, and so I probably spend more time working than the average person. Even when I'm not actually being productive on tangible things, I'm either thinking about my businesses, or writing a song in my head, or engaging in self-development in order to further the impact of my work.

It may sound boring to some, but again, I enjoy it because it holds meaning for me.

That being said, even I and people like me need to take real breaks on a regular basis to avoid burnout, take care of our bodies, and ultimately keep our work joyful over the long term. I have one day a week that I try to keep largely free from scheduled work tasks and filled with a healthy dose of restful and rejuvenating activities. This often means going for a hike, heading for a beach or taking my daughter out for dinner. If I do any kind of work on that day, I try to make sure it is creative, fun stuff rather than boring administrative tasks. For example, for the past few years the business of making music has very much taken a back seat to my other passions. But occasionally, on my day off, I devote an hour or so to writing 'microsongs' based on three random words that my Instagram followers suggest. On the day prior, I ask them to 'Gimme 3 Words' in a comment. On my day off, I choose an entry that inspires me, and I have 24 hours to write a 60-second-or-less microsong and record a video of myself playing it. Then, I post it the next morning. This has provided me with a lot of joy. Additionally, it keeps my followers engaged and keeps my creativity sharp.

Spending Money On Joy

One final thing we should discuss in this chapter is whether money can help to bring us happiness and joy. The proverb that 'money cannot buy happiness' has been around in some shape or form since about the mid-1700s. Since then, the connection between money and happiness has been explored extensively. However, I don't think we need science to tell us that living in financial poverty is not easy on the body, mind or soul. When I think back to my most 'brokest' times, I wasn't particularly happy. Struggling to provide the most basic of needs for yourself and your family – let's face it – sucks. It can be one of the greatest challenges to happiness. On the other hand, it has also been shown that wealthy people are just as prone to depression and suicide as the rest of the population. So, what gives?

As you might expect, there is a sweet spot. People with a level of income that comfortably provides the essentials and allows for a few luxuries tend to be happier than those who live in poverty. It would make sense that there is a basic level of income that makes for an acceptable level of happiness. And a little extra spending money can certainly add some joy and spiciness to our lives.

On the other side of that sweet spot is an area that we might call 'mo' money, mo' problems'. With more wealth can come more status, responsibility, pressure and even isolation. It can also bring about trappings of wanting more material things, or defining your self-worth by your net worth.

This being said, there are lots of ways that wealthy people are deriving great joy from and doing great things with their money. As we've said money is a tremendous tool, and can be used to create a lot of good, particularly if it benefits others, creates connection and serves one's purpose. Remember how knowing and working from your sense of purpose can bring you more joy? Imagine if you had a bunch of spare moolah to be able to do work from that purpose!

Even if you don't have a ton of money, if you have a little extra money, think about how you can spend that to increase your joy. And there is nothing wrong with being a little selfish, especially if you don't spend money on yourself very often.

As mentioned earlier, we all have our little hang-ups about money. For me, beliefs and attitudes around money (and work) have been some of the most difficult things to heal in my life. I grew up with somewhat of a scarcity mindset. It's not like we were dirt poor, but for the first ten years of my life, my parents had to scrimp and save, and we didn't have a lot of luxuries. It was not uncommon for me to hear or over-hear my parents say that we couldn't afford this or that. I also have vivid memories of my father doing his taxes grudgingly. These first impressions about money stayed with me through much of my adult life, and it is only recently that I have made big strides in working toward a more joyful relationship with money.

For many years, I could have been considered a 'tightwad'. I would rarely treat myself, and I rarely gave to others. I wasn't so tight that I wouldn't buy my buddy a drink or pick up the check at dinner, but I stressed about whether I could afford to do it, and the whole social contract of buying things for friends made me uncomfortable. Christmas stressed me out. And I think deep down, I didn't feel I deserved to have a big income, and (big surprise) for most of my life, I didn't.

A few years ago, I began to do the work of dismantling these attitudes around money that held me back. And quite frankly, I still have work to do in those areas. However, for the most part, I see now that money can be a positive force if I intend it to be so. I deeply feel that I deserve to have an abundance of money in my life, and I allow myself to feel joy around money.

Sometimes that means spending money on things, and especially experiences, that bring me joy. (Even though I have a better relationship with money, I am still very much a minimalist when it comes to possessions – too much stuff makes me feel weighted down and suffocated!) For example I recently spent the most money I ever have spent on self-development, attending an out-of-town workshop on embodied leadership with Anne Bérubé, and spending two nights in a hotel room. The old me would never have dreamed of spending almost $1000 on a weekend retreat, but I figured many people would spend much more than that on a weekend that would be far less enriching. I still stressed a bit over making the reservations, but I knew I would be better for it and have a bit of R&R as well.

It turned out to be such a joyful weekend, getting to interact with the other participants, exploring authentic ways of being and also enjoying the amenities of the hotel by myself during the downtime, feeling like a spiritual rock star. It was one of those things that 'ticked all the boxes' – it was joyful in the moment, it was restful and it set me up with skills to squeeze more out of life in the future, *including* lessons that I have brought forward with me and that increase my value to my readers and clients, so that I have the potential to make more money!

So, sometimes you really have to let go a little bit and spend money on joyful things. Ultimately, money cannot buy the 'happily-ever-after' brand of happiness that we tore a strip off of in Chapter 2. But when used in a mindful way, money can help bring little pockets of joy that, over time, can contribute to a holistic sense of joy. As the popular Internet phrase goes 'You are a ghost, driving a meat-coated skeleton, made from stardust, riding a rock, hurtling through space.' You deserve a little treat now and then.

chapter 9

Archetypal Paths to Joy

I can't remember when I first learned the word 'archetype,' but it has captured my imagination and been a fascination of mine for many years. An archetype is representation of a person or thing that is the ideal or prototypical embodiment of that type of person or thing. Huh? OK, it is one of those words that can be a little fuzzy without an example. Let's look at the archetype of 'healer'. The healer archetype envelops all that there is to being a healer, or the 'first form' of a healer. It is a symbolic, ideal representation. A doctor, nurse and physiotherapist are all individual examples of roles that fall under the archetype of healer, but the archetype is all of them rolled up into one.

I feel that, even though our journeys toward happiness and joyfulness are unique and individualized, there are archetypal behaviours and activities we all do that bring us joy. We've already discussed three big archetypes that can potentially bring us a more joyful life: purpose, work and money. But let's take a look at some of the other archetypal paths to joy.

Spirituality/Religion

Legend has it that a reporter once asked Albert Einstein, 'What is the most important question that a scientist can ask?' After much deliberation, Einstein is thought to have answered, 'The most important question that any person can ask is whether or not the universe is a friendly place.' He then said that those who believe it is not friendly are more likely to spend their time and energy building walls and those who believe it is friendly are more likely to build bridges.

I believe that one of the main benefits of healthy spiritual or religious practise is that it can offer us hope that the universe is a friendly place. This faith does not have to come from a traditional view of an external God, who may be friendly or unfriendly (though it might if that's your cup of tea). It can also come from a spiritual understanding of science.

The realization that the universe is a friendly place came to me after studying the biochemistry of energy production in cells, specifically the processes of glycolysis and the Krebs cycle. Don't worry, I won't get too deep into this, and to be honest I've forgotten a lot of the details, but what's important is the meaning behind it.

It all started with the second law of thermodynamics, which basically states that everything tends toward disorder (aka entropy), or in other words, everything breaks down. It actually refers specifically to heat transfer from a warmer thing to a colder thing, but it can also be extrapolated to apply to the breakdown of substances over time. Iron rusts, food decays, dead bodies decay, everything...decays. Well, that's depressing. Sounds pretty unfriendly actually. How does that translate to a friendly universe?

Well, here's where the mystery of life comes in.

Glycolysis and the Krebs cycle are two of the main metabolic pathways that our cells use to liberate energy by breaking down glucose in order to form ATP, an energy carrier that can lend its energy to fuel all the processes in our body, from protein synthesis to muscle contractions to brain function... everything! Our DNA uses this energy to build our bodies, and we use the energy to do the amazing things we do. This is a creative function that opposes the natural tendency toward disorder/entropy.

Now, in the process, glucose is broken down by our cells much faster than it would decay naturally. So basically, our cells are kind of like an engine that *speed up entropy in order to use it against itself.* In other words, life uses destruction in order to create. We eat things, speed up their decay and use that energy to create order (or to fight decay). Isn't that a trip?

So the question of 'life, the universe and everything' is, if the universe is happily coasting toward disorder, what is the creative force that turns this disorder against itself in order to create more order? Well, that to me is Consciousness. That is God. The Big Kahuna. Every tree, every blade of grass, every slime mold, every dragonfly, every one of you, is filled with a consciousness that does this – turning disorder into creation. And maybe that is where joy ultimately comes from: the creation of things that were not there before, the interplay between destruction and creation, and the 'building of bridges' between you as a creative force and all the other creative forces in the universe.

No matter what you believe, taking time to celebrate and be in awe of the beauty of creation can be a fantastic trigger for joy in your life. Honouring Spirit, being thankful to Spirit, even being in communication with Spirit, whatever form that takes for you – these are ways that many people choose as an archetypal path to joy and happiness. And it seems to work. In a 2012 review of over 300 peer-reviewed studies, almost 80% of those studies found only significant positive associations between religiosity/spirituality and well-being. (Koenig, 2012)

Of course, if you don't feel it, you don't feel it. But if you are in a place where you are not feeling a lot of joy, it may be worth taking a look at what you believe about the nature and creativity of the universe. Is it a friendly place? Is there a higher power that you can try to connect with on a more personal level? Is there a sense of wonder and awe that you can tap into? Can you feel amazed that there is order amidst the chaos?

Spiritual faith and practise can also lead you to investigate your inner landscape, to become more familiar with what is uniquely *you*, to find out what it is that truly lights you up. It can also give you an appreciation for and a sense of contentment with the present moment, an ability to more comfortably just *be*. This deeper awareness and peace can also be a fertile ground for joy to grow.

For many people, especially in traditional religions but also in modern spiritual communities, spirituality can be something that is practised in communion with other people, and can therefore enhance our sense of belonging. For me personally, my spirituality was mainly a solitary pursuit for many years, but now I am swinging back the other way and finding that I want to share it with others. Looking back on my childhood religion, even though there are parts that I shunned, I can't deny that there were some pretty joyful moments singing harmonies and playing guitar in that church choir. That shared sense of reverence and celebration among a congregation leads us nicely to our next archetypal path to joy.

Family and Friendship

As mentioned earlier, mystics and physicists alike have told us that the boundaries between us as individuals and our surroundings are fuzzy at best. And it can be said that finding and strengthening our sense of connection to others and to nature may be one of our purest paths to joy. Look at how strong our drive is to find love, whether that be romantic or platonic. Think about the holidays we spend cherishing (and sometimes fighting with) our families. Consider the fierceness and sanctity of the bond between a mother and her child. How about your 'ride or die' bestie?

Personal relationships can provide us with some of the greatest and most intense joys we can ever experience. They can be very complicated as well—the people who bring us the most joy can also bring us the most heartache and pain. In some cases, going through hardship together can bring people closer. I know that my best friends tend to be the ones

I went through tough times with. We can look back on times that seemed the most difficult and see that there was great joy there as well. And in the good times, sharing joy with others can multiply the joy that we feel.

We have already noted that giving to others can be a source of joy. For many people, Dr. Gary Chapman's 5 Love Languages° have become almost household words: we can express affection through words of affirmation, acts of service, gifts, physical touch and quality time. What better way to foster joy in yourself than to give in these ways to someone you love? It's a win-win. Try to think of ways you can give a little extra or carve out a bit of time to spend with family or friends. If you are an organized type and enjoy giving yourself a score, you might even look at the few most important relationships in your life and evaluate how you do each week with each person.

Now, for some of us, getting joy from our relationships with family and friends is relatively easy, but for others it can be downright frustrating and maddening. I had a brief exchange a few months ago with a young man who was very despondent, deeply depressed and anxious, lonely and desperately wanting to have more friends but having very little luck. His attitude was one of complete hopelessness. He couldn't see himself as worthy of having friends. And unfortunately, with that attitude he was only shooting himself in the foot and pushing away any potential friendships with his 'poor me', sad sack persona. Again, 'If you don't love yourself, how in the hell you gonna love somebody else?'

For some, the road to having joyful relationships with

family and friends begins with a long journey of internal work to be able to love themselves and have a core of internal joy first. However, if they are able to get past their inner demons enough to choose joy for themselves, their family and friends can be a path to maintaining and enriching that core joy.

Arts and Sciences

As I have shared bits and pieces of my personal joy journey, you have no doubt picked up that exploring the world through the arts and sciences has played a large role in my life, as it has for billions of people around the world. Life is a giant mystery that is continually unfolding in ways both expected and unexpected, and art and science are ages-old methods for trying to make sense of this mystery, subjectively and objectively. Both can be very deep paths to joy.

Art can be used to express and celebrate joy, but also to heal and transform its opposite: emotional pain. This healing can come both from producing art and from consuming it. How many times have you heard someone say about a musical artist, 'Their music saved my life'? This is an example of the tremendous power that art can have in transforming us. It is a form of deep emotional communication and helps us to connect with others in universally understandable ways. Through its symbolism, art often speaks to us of archetypes – mothers and fathers, lovers, heroes, tricksters, lovable losers and sages – sometimes subconsciously teaching us about ourselves.

Art can even affect our moods, seemingly without any

effort or thought on our part. Looking at a beautiful painting or listening to a favourite piece of music can immediately make you feel better. Creating your own art can bring an even deeper and longer lasting joy, particularly if you do it for yourself and are not overly concerned about how it is 'supposed to be' or how other people would judge it. As I have already mentioned, finishing writing a song or playing a great show bring me some of the most exciting feelings I ever experience.

Also, art does not have to be grandiose or 'high art' to be joyful. Crafts and all sorts of creative hobbies can bring us the same kind of joy. I know a successful singer-songwriter who, as a pandemic project, built an elaborate slot racing village, complete with a drive-in movie for the little cars to attend. He obviously derived a lot of pleasure and pride from it, as did we who follow him on social media. How much joy has come from the hands of knitters and woodworkers and bakers and potters as their creations are given or sold to others to warm their homes and bodies?

If you are feeling low, try bringing a bit more art in your life, anything from having a dance party in your kitchen, to going to see live theatre, to taking a graffiti tour of your neighbourhood.

Perhaps less common in the daily life of our culture but nonetheless a powerful path to joy is science. For many people, answering questions about the world around us is a great source of happiness. Curiosity seems to be one of our core traits as human beings, and is something that likely starts to develop even before birth, but certainly shortly after it. Infants explore the world around them using their senses, and as we grow we learn to use tools to explore further and deeper. As a species, we have studied a large percentage of our planet and the space billions of miles around it, as well as peering into the miniscule world of elemental particles and energy that make up the fabric of our worldly existence. We never run out of questions. Some quantum physicists are now hinting that our questioning and observing of the quantum field may actually be influencing the behaviour of the basic building blocks of reality.

Psychologists tell us that two of our basic needs are certainty and uncertainty. Science provides us with both. Well-tested theories such as gravity, the basic laws of thermodynamics and Newtonian physics give us a sense of certainty and control. Through understanding these basic laws, we can routinely do things like send our voices and images across continents without a second thought. And yet, there is so much left to learn in every field of endeavour. The workings of our own bodies alone provide us with so many questions to be explored, never mind the vast underwater swaths of our planet that we have yet to visit, the immense galaxies that we cannot yet perceive and the complexity of the subatomic world.

We can find great joy in applying the principles of known science, as well as in studying the unknown using scientific methods. All you have to do to witness that kind of joy is watch a kids' science fair or robotics competition.

As you have probably noticed, science and spirituality are not at odds with each other in my world. I have much reverence for the mysteries of life, and I believe that many things will remain mysterious for a very long time. There are questions around the nature of consciousness that may never be answered by scientific inquiry, but I believe strongly in examining all that we can scientifically and solving as many mysteries as we can using objective experimentation. We are already seeing a tremendous explosion in the amount of serious science being devoted to questions about where consciousness comes from and the mysterious behaviour of matter and energy at the quantum level. While I believe science and spirituality have always been more closely linked than the religious leaders of the past would have us believe, there is now exciting work that is showing how mysteriously *connected* everything is.

I mentioned in Chapter 1 that the word 'joy' has often been seen as the domain of organized religion. Just as in the past people might have been encouraged to 'find joy in God', today many of us may be more inclined to find our joy in a path that still honours mystery and even divinity, but takes a more curiosity-based road to get there.

Nature

One of the most fascinating things about humanity, in my mind, is our puzzling relationship to the natural world. I think it is safe to say that, with the exception of animals we have domesticated, we are the only species that does not live immersed in its natural surroundings. We have used our technology to isolate ourselves from nature, to the extent that we even seek to physically leave the planet, or to create virtual worlds to which we can escape. It actually makes me wonder if we really belong here, but that is a topic for another book!

That being said, there is undoubtedly a part of us that yearns to connect deeply to nature.

As amazing and relatively comfortable as our technologically advanced life can be, it can also be extremely stressful, isolating, hollow and even depressing. For many of us, just stepping into the woods can help us to breathe easier and decompress almost immediately. Recently, on one of the colder days of our Canadian winter, I willed myself to get out for a walk on the dykelands near my home. As tough as it was to face the icy winds at first, within minutes I started to feel a shift inside me. The cold became a minor discomfort as I marvelled at the sound of the few Canada geese who decided not to migrate south this year, and then saw a very early robin who was probably as cold as I was. I took a more sheltered route home, with the wind at my back and the sun on my face, and it now seemed like a glorious day! When I returned home, my spirits were higher, my thoughts were clearer and I felt more ready to tackle my day.

Biologist Edward O. Wilson noted humans' urge to affiliate with other forms of life and called it 'biophilia.' He hypothesized that our desire to connect deeply with nature is a consequence of our evolutionary biology. But he also pointed out that this drive also includes negative or phobic associations with nature. This makes some intuitive sense, in that our ancient ancestors faced many more immediate dangers, in the form of predators and exposure to the elements, than we do today. It can be said that the work of engineering of our environments over millennia has had a lot to do with maximizing our 'positive' interactions with nature and minimizing the 'negative' ones. However, it may be that in elevating our love of technology and its comforts to cult-like status, we are throwing the baby out with the bathwater. Our lack of willingness to get outside and get our hands dirty could be having a detrimental effect on our overall mental and emotional wellness.

On an individual level, you may not have the same excitement for the outdoors as avid hikers, backwoods campers and mountaineers do. And that's just fine! To each their own. However, if you are finding yourself in a depressed state or having difficulty connecting to your joy, getting a bit more fresh air and time out in the sunshine might be just what you need to start building some momentum in your physiology to break out of that rut and into a more joyful state.

Body: Movement, Food and Sex

Whether you believe we are spiritual beings inhabiting a body or that our body is all we are, it is clear that our physical body is the primary vehicle by which we experience life and the world around us. And so, the pleasures that we experience through our body can be a wonderful source of joy.

On my own journey, I spent many years after my depressive period 'just being OK'. The one thing that really brought things together to help me feel joyful again was physical exercise. (The irony that I discovered this 15 years after starting my career in exercise science is not lost on me.) Getting my body moving first thing in the morning feels to me like blowing out the cobwebs. Not only does it feel good from the neck *down*, but even more importantly for me, it primes my mind for the day, making it feel clearer and more alert. My routine during the spring, summer and fall is to run six days a week, first thing in the morning after two glasses of water. There is the occasional day when I don't feel like it, but there is never a day that I don't feel great afterward, and most days I can't wait to get outside and get moving. During the winter I switch to yoga, which I have to admit is more difficult for me to get excited about, but I'm also not crazy about running on icy sidewalks and risking cracking my skull open. That said, I do find joy in moving and stretching my body, while focusing on breathing. The slower pace seems to mesh with the quiet winter mornings, and it helps to repair and prepare my body for the seasons of more intense exercise.

Now, many of you might be cringing at the mere thought of exercise, and that's OK. But I will say that our bodies are designed to move, and *especially* if you have issues with low moods, regular exercise is practically a miracle in terms of shifting your baseline mood profile upward without rebound effects. Try to find something that is fun for you, something that gets you moving without you having to force yourself or think too hard about it. You don't have to do a lot – every little bit helps, and something is better than nothing.

Whether or not exercise is your thing, when talking about the body we also need to talk about food. What a source of joy food can be! It is no coincidence that most of our celebrations and holidays have a big focus on food. From growing it to shopping for it, preparing it and the eating it, food can be a sensual experience of colours, aromas, textures, sounds and of course tastes. Unsurprisingly, one of the most famous cookbooks of all time is called *The Joy of Cooking*. For a lot of us, food is a very direct path to joy.

Unfortunately, for many others, food is a source of distress, pain, shame and struggle. And even on a cultural level, we have seen our relationship to food become more distanced, corporatized, sped up and devalued. In the process, sadly, much of the joy around food has been lost or perverted. While I don't want to dwell on these negative trends around our relationship with food, I want to explain what I mean when I say that our joy around food has been 'perverted'.

In our evolutionary history, the taste of food generally gave us an indication of what we should and should not eat. For the most part, with some exceptions, in nature, things that are good for us taste good and things that are bad for us taste bad. In times when food was more scarce, sugars and fats in particular were preferred by our taste buds. Sugar would give us immediate energy to, say, run from a sabre-toothed tiger, and fats gave us sustained energy and could be stored against future scarcity. We now know that in natural, whole foods, those sugars and fats are bundled with a plethora of beneficial vitamins, minerals, proteins, enzymes and micronutrients that make a complete, synergistic package. As such, the joy that we feel from eating whole foods is a deep joy that comes from nourishing our bodies the way nature intended.

In today's corporatized food landscape, we have many foods that are processed, in many cases with large amounts of added simple sugars and fats to make them taste good, They often have synthetic vitamins added back in, but lack the enzymes and micronutrients of whole foods. And the joy that we feel in eating some of these foods is practically indistinguishable from when we eat whole foods. I'm not going to lie—every once in a while, a fast food burger and fries tastes mightily good. But an hour after eating them, I tend to feel lethargic and queasy.

This is the 'perversion' I am speaking of: food that feels good in the moment but does very little to support our greater joy. There is a quick hit of sugar and fat that tickles the ancient part of our brain, but there is a tremendous lack of nutritional value and longer-term benefit. There's nothing wrong with the odd treat of course, but making a habit of enjoying whole, healthy foods regularly is a much better path to sustainable core joy, especially if those foods are lovingly prepared and shared with people you love.

As with the other forms of bodily pleasure, sex is an avenue to joy that also has potential for all sorts of difficulties.

Approached mindfully and with a level of reverence, sex can be one of the most joyful things we do as human beings. It is, after all, the way that we came into this world, our ultimate creative act. It is a way to show and celebrate love, not to mention a pure and simple pleasure. And yet, it can also be fraught with intense emotional pain and distress.

Sex is a sensitive topic, and it is not my intention to get too deep into it, but I think it's fair to say that sex has become perverted in our culture (and not in the good way). It has been put on a pedestal, something to be watched, fetishized (also not in the good way) and glorified for profit. Unreasonable expectations are placed on people of all genders and orientations, to the point where many people avoid sexuality altogether, or end up with any number of unhealthy hang-ups, habits and obsessions.

Nevertheless, if you can avoid the pitfalls of today's 'pornucopia' and can manage to be authentically yourself and find a special person or persons to be authentically yourself with, sexuality can be a very powerful archetypal path to joy.

Pets

This one's a no-brainer, isn't it?

It was once estimated that cats drive about 15% of internet traffic. Culture writer Maria Bustillos (2015) wrote, 'Cat videos are the crystallization of all that human beings love about cats, the crux of which is centred in the fact that cats are both beautiful and absurd. Their natural beauty and majesty are eternally just one tiny slip away from total humiliation, and this precarious condition fills us with a sympathetic panic and delight, for it exactly mirrors our own.'

And let's not even talk about those goofy, slobbering love-bombs that we call dogs.

They're not for everybody, but those who like them, like them a lot. When I come home from a tough day, nothing cheers me up more than giving my Sphynx cat a kiss on her wrinkly little forehead, or cuddling her follicly gifted brother and sister.

Pets give us the gift of tremendous joy for the low, low price of room and board and a bit of care. They become part of our families and touch our hearts. It might be said that it is an extension of our connection to nature, our 'biophilia', but for those of us who enjoy having pets in our lives, it is much more than that. It is a bond of unconditional love.

'Nuff said.

Play

When we are children, play is one of the most natural ways for us to experience and express joy. And while our sense of play changes as we mature, it is still an important part of our lives in terms of helping us sharpen skills, use creative thinking, stay fit and recuperate from our work. Role playing, games of skill (both physical and mental), dance and sports are some of the ways that we play as adults. Having kids around can also get us back in touch with freer, more creative forms play as well.

Play is one of our first paths to joy in our development, and it occurs in other animals as well, which suggests that it may be the most fundamental archetype of joyful behaviour. As such, play can be a synergistic component of the other paths – we can play with Spirit, we play with our friends and family, we play in nature, we play when we exercise, we play with our food, we play sexually, we play with our pets. We play, we have fun, we foster joy. So get out there and play more!

Your Secondary Joy Choices

In Chapter 3, we explored how we can actually *choose* to be joyful. Making this choice can be a one-time event – that moment where you take charge and say 'I have faith in my sustainable, core joy from now on, even when things are hard.' That is indeed a momentous occasion, and a tremendous win for your life.

However, in order for it to stick, that choice has to be supported by your other, smaller choices. I call these 'secondary joy choices.' These choices are often to do with the archetypal paths to joy we have been examining in this chapter. For example, my choice to run or do yoga six days a week is a secondary choice that supports my choice to live in joy because it boosts my baseline mood, keeps my body healthy, gives me time outdoors and gives me a positive start to my day.

You could choose to drink a fruit smoothie every morning because it tastes great and is good for you. You could choose to adopt a dog to help support your mental health and because it will get you out walking. You might choose to look for a job that better aligns with your sense of purpose because it will be more fulfilling and less stressful.

Secondary joy choices are the real meat and potatoes of the choice to be more joyful. The initial choice—to say definitively from this moment forward, 'I choose joy'—is an amazing step, but it is only the beginning. Whether or not that decision has meaning and staying power is largely based on making choices every day that support this journey.

These choices do not have to, and probably should not, come all at once. If you try to leap all at once into eating whole foods, exercising every day, meditating, deep cleaning your house and repairing all your relationships, you will probably get overwhelmed, burn out and give up. But making small achievable shifts, celebrating your progress and building upon it will put you on the path to success.

When you start to be more consistent in making secondary joy choices that support your core joy, you will start to notice a kind of efficiency in your life. This is because the activities you are engaged in are working together in a holistic network. Your good food choices work together with your joyful physical activity choices to make you healthier and more fit. Your fitness supports your choice to be a better lover for your partner. Your more joyful relationship makes you better parents. Your happy home life helps to make you a better employee or entrepreneur. In this way, joy can become a guiding principle that creates efficiency and more successes in every area of your life.

chapter 10

Flow and Mindfulness

In the zone. In the groove. 'Forgetting to eat and poop'. Psychologist Mihaly Csikszentmihalyi called this type of immersive focus 'the flow state,' and it has become one of the core theories in the field of positive psychology. When we are in flow, we tend to forget our worries, we feel time speed up or slow down (or become practically meaningless), our focus sharpens and we feel like we are fully engaged in what we are doing. Flow can present us with almost effortless success, and a sense of losing ourselves in an activity. Our normal mental chatter falls away. We become one with what we are doing.

Flow usually comes when a task is optimally challenging—that is, if it is not too easy as to be boring and not too difficult as to be frustrating. Even though I'm not much of a video game player, I must admit that video games provide one of the most relatable examples of flow. Think about a multi-level game which gets progressively harder as you advance through the levels. When you are first learning the basics of the game, you might not get into a flow state at all. Even the first few levels might be so challenging that they are frustrating. You might get on a brief roll but then die unexpectedly because of some wrinkle that you didn't understand. But then, at some point, the initial levels become second nature, the middle levels are just challenging enough to be exciting and the final levels are maybe still frustrating and just out of reach. It is at this point, when you are crushing the challenging parts in the middle and have a reasonable chance of beating the higher levels, that you are most likely to get into a flow state.

For me, as a songwriter, flow usually comes once I have a few critical pieces of a new song, like the chord progression and the chorus, and I have a good idea of where the song is 'going'. Then I'm off to the races, as they say. I can be working on it for hours and then suddenly look up and realize that it's dark outside and I am ravenous.

Getting into the flow state more often is thought by many to correlate with greater happiness. This is a matter of some debate among academics, and it has been said that Csikszentmihalyi himself seems 'not too happy with the idea that his theory of flow has been taken to be a theory of happiness' (Krueger, 2015). Nevertheless, I feel that flow experiences, especially healthy, wholesome ones, tend to be joyful experiences and can contribute to our baseline of happiness.

Csikszentmihalyi once said, 'The best moments in our lives are not the passive, receptive, relaxing times – although such experiences can also be enjoyable, if we have worked hard to attain them. The best moments usually occur when a person's body or mind is stretched to its limits in a voluntary effort to accomplish something difficult and worthwhile' (Csikszentmihalyi, 1990). If being in flow equates to some of the best moments in our lives, then surely stringing together more of those types of moments contributes to our sense of sustainable core joy.

So, can we, and how do we get into flow more consciously, rather than just leaving it to chance?

In addition to doing something that is optimally challenging as mentioned earlier, there are a few important qualities to the types of activities that are more likely to get you into flow. First, it should be something that you care about. The more invested you are in the activity, the more likely you are to become fully engrossed in it. Second, it should be something that you are proficient at. Like our video game example, if you are in the beginning stages of learning something, your focus may be somewhat fragmented because you need to process a lot of negative feedback and make a lot of adjustments. It may not be particularly exciting, because you are not meeting with a lot of success. When you have a certain level of proficiency, part of your skill set can be on autopilot and you can focus on the finer details that lead you to more and more success. Finally, your mindset during the task should be on the activity itself rather than the end goal. The end is a future event, and focusing on that future is not conducive to being immersed and engaged in the present moment. For a musician, this might mean focusing on their bandmates and the current moment in the song, as opposed to how the audience will react at the end. For an athlete, it might mean focusing on the game rather than on the win.

While I believe that getting into the flow state periodically is good for us and has potential for increasing our joy, it is not something that we can sustain. We cannot and probably would not want to be in flow all the time. After all, we have to eat and poop sometime, right?

There is, however, a cousin to flow that we talked about earlier, which can be a relatively consistent state of mind and can foster joy in a big way, and that is mindfulness. Mindfulness, according to mindful.org (which I highly recommend), 'is the basic human ability to be fully present, aware of where we are and what we're doing, and not overly reactive or overwhelmed by what's going on around us.'

Whereas in flow we are completely immersed in what we are *doing*, in mindfulness we are equally present in *being*. It is a basic awareness of ourselves, our mind and our body. It is us paying attention. And, with practise, it can become a greater and greater part of our day-to-day consciousness.

The mindful person is vigilantly aware of their feelings, thoughts, actions and reactions. They know that, even though things happen that are beyond their control, they ultimately shape their destiny by the ways in which they view and react to the people, places and events in their world.

The mindful person keeps a close eye on their mind-garden, carefully tending it, nourishing it and loving it so that it is a better place to live. They try to remember that they themselves are a part of the Divine, and so are worthy of self-acceptance and self-love.

The mindful person might ask themselves questions like, 'How can I create and spread more joy today?' or 'How might

I serve others today?' or 'How do I stay more present for my family today?' At the end of their day, they might review how the day went or even evaluate themselves on how well they were able to do the things they set out to do.

The thing that I have learned about mindfulness is that it is like a muscle that you train. When we first get the idea that we want to be more mindful, we have likely been on a sort of auto-pilot. Our thoughts and our feelings have always just kind of done what they do, often until we realize that we are having a lot of unwanted thoughts. Questioning our unwanted thoughts can be both liberating and frightening, because we begin to realize that there is a 'speaker' and a 'listener' in our minds. And sometimes the speaker says things that aren't cool! Then we can ask ourselves, if I am not controlling my thoughts, then who is?

For many people, that question is terrifying, but it doesn't have to be that way. We take in information constantly, and it is our mind's job to process that information, filtering out what is unimportant and integrating the important stuff with our existing system of values and beliefs. Some of this processing is done consciously, but because we have so many things happening all at once in our lives, some is done subconsciously, both while we are awake and while we are asleep.

With so much going on, I believe it is inevitable that the odd bit of unwanted or unhealthy programming will slip its way in. We live in a world where we are constantly surrounded by images and sounds, many that are purposefully presented in ways that try to command our attention and get us to buy what is being sold. Hell, I can still remember the ingredients to a Big Mac from a song that I learned from TV in the 1980s! The point is that there are people out there trying to influence your thoughts – that is a given. But when you begin to really spend time being in your 'listener' self, you can start to hear and discern which types of thoughts you want to live with every day.

The early part of mindfulness training is just that – paying more attention to the quality of your thoughts throughout the day and just noticing them, without judging yourself. If you notice yourself say in your head, 'I'm so lazy', don't make it worse by admonishing yourself, just recognize that you had that thought: 'Hmm, it's interesting that I thought that.'

After a few weeks of this, once you feel like you are becoming more mindful of the thoughts that you have, you can start to gently redirect them on a better course. For example, if you catch yourself thinking, 'I'm so lazy', you can say, 'Well, OK, I'm not lazy all the time. I'm just feeling a bit unmotivated right now. What are some little things I could do to change that? Do I need to rest? Is there a small task I can do to give myself a sense of accomplishment? Would doing something for someone else make me feel better about myself?'

Sometimes, if you know there are persistent limiting thoughts that you struggle with and that show up time and again, you can have a few affirmations at the ready for when they pop up. Personally, I have some blocks around being entrepreneurial, and will sometimes have thoughts such as 'I'm not a people person' or 'Marketing sucks' or 'Why would anyone want to buy this?' And so, I have affirmations that I say to myself, such as 'I am a charismatic boss', 'I am not afraid of failure, because entrepreneurs sometimes fail their way to success' and 'My products and services deliver tremendous value to many people, and I am compensated accordingly.'

It is just as important to try and make the words you speak out loud be a representation of your truth and your positive intentions. The practise of speaking things aloud is very powerful. You might know someone in your circle of acquaintances who is always complaining about *something*. 'I'm so broke. The weather is so crap. My car is on the fritz again. I hate my boss.' The spoken word is literally vibrations. When we put out a 'bad vibe', we are likely to attract things that are on the same frequency.

I am fortunate to live in a community of people who are pretty mindful of the words they speak into existence. But if your circle of friends would look at you like you had two heads if you said something positive, maybe they are not the best friends, or maybe you can practise making affirmations out loud to yourself alone, until you are ready to have the courage to introduce your friends to this way of being, thinking and speaking.

As your mindfulness muscles grow, you may start to find yourself in a more joyful environment in your mind. Furthermore, you might want to start specifically being mindful of your 'joy level'. I quite often check in with myself to make sure I'm tuned in to my core joy. Am I living as joyfully as possible, even when I have unpleasant tasks to do, or am I not feeling physically up to par? Am I doing all I can to spread joy to other people? This can be challenging, and I am far from perfect at carrying it out. I often 'wake up' and realize I've been on a less-than-joyful autopilot for a while. That stuff happens. But even when I am, say, having a heated discussion with my bestie, I try to stay mindful and make sure that I am speaking from an authentic, loving and non-reactive place, even though we're both a little angry with each other.

At some point, hopefully, you will begin to find that your 'listener' self is much more at ease with what your 'speaker' self is prattling on about all day, and that your thoughts are more in alignment with your goals, values and beliefs. You will also be properly focused on the past, present or future at appropriate times and in reasonable proportions, as we discussed in Chapter 4. You'll spend most of your energy focusing on the present and the future, while relying on lessons of the past to help you move forward confidently.

Eventually, mindfulness may become a new kind of auto-pilot, where you are effortlessly putting forward a more thoughtful, engaged, grounded, authentic and joyful self. (Hopefully, even I will get there someday! But life is a journey, isn't it?) When mindfulness becomes your default, you can become your own biggest supporter and cheerleader, and put yourself in a much better place to be the same for others. You can love yourself more fully and open yourself up to more love with others. You can focus more clearly on your purpose, reach more confidently for success, however you define it, and cultivate more happiness and joy in your life.

chapter 11

Getting Through the Tough Times

I t is often believed that the Buddha said, 'Life is suffering.'
Now isn't that depressing? Fortunately however, this is a
case of meaning being lost in translation. In the Pali language
that he spoke, he would have said 'Life is *dukkha*.' *Dukkha*
can be seen as a three-fold concept that includes:

1. Suffering, pain or dissatisfaction
2. Impermanence or change (i.e. everything, including
   suffering and happiness, is impermanent)
3. All things being interdependent

If we look at Buddha's teaching from this expanded perspective, we can say that, as we navigate this world of matter
and energy with free will, interacting with other beings
who have free will, we will inevitably suffer at times. However, that suffering will be impermanent, and how much
we suffer depends largely on how we react to our suffering.

Furthermore, and somewhat ironically, it is often in the avoidance of suffering that we suffer the most. In trying to create a 'perfect', pain-free life, we can fall into addiction to soothing behaviours such as drug abuse, overeating and compulsive sex that can lead us to more pain over time.

So, how do we navigate the difficult times without spiralling into depression, chronic anxiety or addiction, and while maintaining faith in our core of joy?

This is where the rubber meets the road, as they say. It is easy to remember our joy when things are going well, but yet another to be able to remain connected to joy when shit hits the fan.

The first thing to remember is to feel your authentic feelings. If you feel sad, you need to sit in your sadness and make space for it. This is not about faking joyfulness or glossing over your suffering. It's about really feeling whatever it is you need to feel, yet knowing at the deepest level that joy is your true essence, and that it is always there waiting for you.

If you try to 'fake it till you make it' by pretending everything is rainbows and roses, you may as well be doing drugs to numb the pain, because you are just ignoring it and stuffing it down. Sooner or later it is bound to catch up with you.

Now, while we do want to deal with the feelings surrounding our hardships, we also need some strategies to make sure that those feelings don't overwhelm us and that joy never gets pushed too far to the back burner.

1. Do not wallow. Remember that our suffering and our happiness are impermanent. Treat your emotions as though they are visitors. Some will need to stay with us longer than others, of course. Emotions around a major loss or tragedy will need your attention for a long time, and will probably be repeat visitors. But with any feeling, try to avoid wallowing in it. This was a difficult lesson for me. I used to stretch out my negative emotional states much longer than was necessary. If I was criticized unfairly by a lover, I would sometimes mope for days with hurt feelings, even after I had aired them out. I was (consciously or unconsciously) trying to punish the other person, but I was also punishing myself by being in a crappy mood for longer than I should have been. Wallowing is a waste of time and a killer of long-term joy.

2. Make sure the magnitude of your emotional response fits the situation. A related strategy is to check in with yourself and make sure that your emotional responses to difficult circumstances 'fit the crime'. Take a step back and try to gauge as objectively as you can whether you might be 'catastrophizing' your situation. Is it really worthy of all the stress and internal anguish?

I have a neighbour who is getting up there in years and is not able to get out much, but she has a nice old house and a decent support system of family, friends and neighbours. She spends a lot of time watching the news and the weather channel. Every time there is even a moderate snow, rain or wind storm forecast, she goes on and on about 'what a horrible storm is coming'. Now, I know for a fact that in her 70-odd years of Canadian living, she has survived dozens of wicked storms that would make your head spin, because I've lived a considerably shorter life and have seen many myself. And yet, she tortures herself worrying about minor weather events that barely amount to anything. (At this point I will digress from launching into a rant about how television news is a tool to keep people living in fear!)

What are some of the 'horrible storms' that you worry yourself over that may not actually be so horrible?

Worry itself is not a bad thing – in proper proportion and balance, it keeps us sharp and focuses our energy toward problem-solving. As I often tell clients, however, you have to be careful about where you 'spend your worry bucks'!

3. Keep your gratitude habit going. When things get tough, don't forget the Big G. During these times it may be harder to feel grateful, but times of suffering are the most important time to keep a habit of gratitude. Even if, God forbid, you have recently lost a loved one or lost a great job or suffered a serious injury, finding things to be grateful for and expressing that gratitude will ultimately get you to a better place sooner than you would otherwise. During these times when it seems like there is little to be thankful for, try getting down to basics. Be thankful for the people you have, be thankful for your breath, be thankful for the sun. It may even be difficult to feel authentic while you are doing it, but just keeping up the habit will be healing.

4. Remember joyful times and feelings. When I am suffering, I often find it useful to practise mindfulness meditation to recall joyful times and feelings. I see this as a kind of reminder that I have felt joy in the past and that I will feel joy in the future. I sit quietly and take a few deep breaths, then recall a joyful event and just hold on to the feeling. When I notice the feeling start to fade, I gently bring it back into my attention. I will continue to do this for five minutes or so, and then choose one or two more memories to hang on to for five minutes each, for a total of a 10 or 15-minute mediation. You don't need to go that long, or you can go longer if you wish.

Notice that this is different than trying to fake it till you make it. You are not trying to gloss over your suffering or put on a fake smile for hours or days at a time. You are simply remembering joy in a deliberate, conscious way for a little while. You are still honouring and working through your difficult feelings, but you are taking time out to remind yourself of their impermanence and of your joyful core.

5. *Focus on positive outcomes for the future.* Just as recalling joyful events from your past can remind you of your innate joy, envisioning positive circumstances for your future can remind you that all things are impermanent and that joy will return in its full manifestation. Try getting yourself in a state of 'pronoia' – the opposite of paranoia, where you believe that everything is conspiring to do you good. Visualize yourself doing things that make you feel purposeful, alive, productive and joyful. Try to not only see it, but hear it, smell it, taste it and feel it. Make it as real as possible and, like in the previous exercise, when you notice it start to fade, just gently bring it back into focus and repeat as long as you like.

6. Don't go it alone. I believe that part of why I lingered in depression for many years is that I didn't share enough with others. This can be extremely challenging, as the lowered self-esteem that often accompanies depression and other extended hardships can cause us to isolate ourselves. We don't want to be a burden on others and we don't feel like anyone could possibly understand what we are going through. The fact is that most people want to help others, and the friendships that are forged in shared struggle are often the greatest friendships you will ever experience. The people who want to share in your joy, more often than not, will also want to support you in your times of suffering. Wouldn't you do the same for them? There is no need to let false pride or martyrdom keep you from getting help in properly processing difficult emotions. As Ram Dass said, 'We are all just walking each other home.'

7. Connect to a higher power. Feelings such as anxiety and depression often come from, or at least are compounded by, the sense that you have to do everything for yourself. Connecting to a higher power can help you to feel that you are never completely alone, that there is a force that is bigger than all of us there to support you through everything. As you connect more and more to this energy, you may even come to realize that this mysterious higher power that exists in and works through all of us is not only a source of strength, but the ultimate source of all our joys.

Here, I'm going to go on a brief tangent, but I promise it will circle back to the main topic of this chapter.

Where does joy reside within us? Our imagination and the metaphors of our literary, mystical and religious history would tell us that joy lives *in the heart*. Additionally, we live in an amazing time, when we are beginning to see more and more coherence between our mystical imaginations and scientific thought. A case in point is that science is beginning to investigate the role that our *physical* heart plays in our emotional responses. Previously thought to be a rather mechanical organ that simply pumped blood throughout the body, scientists are now considering the possibility that the heart may actually be 'intelligent' and integral to our emotional processes.

This research is in its infancy, and some of it has been criticized as being pseudoscientific, so at this point I would prescribe a few grains of salt to go with it, but just consider the potential implications of this for a moment. Traditionally, our emotions have been thought to arise primarily through interactions of the frontal lobe and limbic system. Thus, science has long held that emotions come from our brains. Our sympathetic and parasympathetic nervous systems then tell our heart and other organs whether to speed up or slow down. However, like most systems in our bodies, this is not just a one-way street. Our heart sends feedback to our brains in an ongoing communication loop, to ensure that our body is ready for either 'fight or flight' or 'rest and repair' or somewhere in between.

The folks who are studying the intelligence of the heart,

such as the HeartMath Institute, claim that the information sent from the heart to the brain is more complex than previously thought. They suggest that 'the heart communicates with the brain and body in four ways: neurological communication (nervous system), biochemical communication (hormones), biophysical communication (pulse wave) and energetic communication (electromagnetic fields)' (https://www.heartmath.org/research/science-of-the-heart/heart-brain-communication/). They suggest that our heart rate does not always follow precisely the input of the autonomic nervous signals from the brain, but appears to be 'behaving as though it had a mind of its own. Furthermore, the heart appeared to be sending meaningful messages to the brain that the brain not only understood, but also obeyed. Even more intriguing was that it looked as though these messages could affect a person's perceptions, behaviour and performance.'

If this is true, then our heart (and perhaps even other internal organs) work in concert with our brain to create emotions. And so, our joy may actually live, at least in part, in our hearts.

Additionally, our heart actually transmits a much larger electromagnetic field than that of the brain. The researchers at HeartMath are even investigating how our own heart might influence other people's hearts and brains, giving new meaning to emotional states such as joy being 'infectious'!

So, what does this idea of joy residing in our hearts have to do with getting through the tough times?

It has to do with faith and reliability. The heart is 'at the heart' of the physical core of our being. It is the organ that we can rely on to keep on beating day in and day out, without our conscious control. Our mind may drift and change, sometimes on a dime, even if we are practised at mediation and mindfulness. But our heart carries the memory and promise of joy always, without fail. So, in our trying times, if we can remember that our heart is the reservoir for our core joy, we can have absolute faith that joy will always come back to us.

The heart, too, is much older than the self-conscious mind. And for that reason, we can lean on its wisdom, which is drawn from eons of living in harmony with the earth, water, fire, air, the sun, the moon and the unseen universe. Its joy runs deep, and that joy feeds us, even when our conscious mind is running in circles and feeling low.

Take a moment now to check in with your heart. Sit quietly and take a few deep breaths. Then, turn your attention to your heart and feel the energy surrounding it. Is it easy and bright? Or is it tight and dark? Or somewhere in between? Sit with that feeling a while and really pay attention to it. Don't worry about trying to analyze what it means or what brought your heart to this state. It doesn't matter right now. It's in the past. Just feel the feeling of it.

Now, imagine a light coming from above you and bathing your heart. Breathe the light into your heart, and breathe out the tension. See if your heart gets brighter and lighter. (It helps to smile while you do this!)

Doing this exercise makes it clear that joy is not just in our brain, and that our heart may actually be joy's physical, and not just metaphorical home. The other thing this exercise shows is that we can, to a certain extent, 'hack' our bodies and minds to feel more joy in a matter of minutes. And with practise, this can become very natural, so that, when we inevitably go through *dukkha,* an impermanent, circumstance-based suffering, we can feel the suffering for as long as we need to, but then we can consciously choose to shift our physiology and our psychology back toward joy.

chapter 12

Faith

In the previous chapter, I briefly alluded to the concept of faith. I believe that faith is one of the cornerstones of a core joy mindset, so let's discuss it a bit further.

When I was a young person coming up in the institutions of church and school, the word faith was usually applied to an external 'sky Daddy' God. We were instructed to have faith that God had a plan for us, and that whatever we were going through was all part of the plan. We just had to be good and follow the rules and everything would work out fine. And there's nothing wrong with believing that – my grandparents were two of the most joyful people I have ever known, and they had tremendous faith in God, in the traditional Catholic sense.

But for many of us, that version of God seemed too simplistic or too impersonal. We wondered why God's plan included such atrocities and unfairness. We searched outwardly and inwardly, stumbled around in the dark, suffered broken hearts, faced our fears and came out the other side with a deeper, personal understanding of the universal consciousness. For me, the journey through the dark night of the soul led me to a realization that we are all a small part of God—a spark of God, if you will, rather than something separate. Our consciousness is a microcosm of the vast consciousness that is everything – we are 'the ocean.' We are here to experience ourselves as seemingly separate egos that are all at once still connected to that higher power.

You might say that there comes a time in many self-development books, audio courses, films or workshops where everything boils down to love and creativity. This is that time for this book.

When you see the world as the constantly unfolding creation of a higher force that *you are actually a part of,* it becomes clear that your purpose here on earth is to love and to create. You will likely refine that purpose to something that is most meaningful to you, but at the core, it's as simple as that – love and create!

When you see the world as the constantly unfolding creation of a higher force that *you are actually a part of,* you will see that you deserve joy. In fact, you will get a palpable sense that joy is your *birthright* and your natural state of being.

When you see the world as the constantly unfolding creation of a higher force that *you are actually a part of,* you realize that atrocities, violence and unfairness manifest themselves when people *forget* they are a part of God, when they *forget* to love and create.

The tough part of course is that we all forget sometimes. It's a part of the human experience. We forget, and we succumb to feelings of fear, ostracism, lack or insecurity. And we do shitty things. And when we see the shitty things that we and other people do, it can be difficult to have faith in that higher power of love and creativity.

Well, nobody said faith was going to be easy. But for me, it is easier to have faith in a higher power that I have an intimate relationship with and am (in a tiny part) responsible for, than an impersonal higher power that plays us like chess pieces. And so, I have faith, not only that the universe will unfold as it should in its imperfect perfection, but also in myself as a force of love and creation within that universe. I have faith especially in my subconscious mind, which I believe stays in firm contact with the love and creativity of higher energies, even when my conscious mind is presenting like a cranky, sad curmudgeon.

You and I are miracles of creation. It has been surmised that the probability of the unique *you* being born was around 1 in 400 trillion. And yet, nature made us with absolute ease, as it has for 200,000 years of *homo sapiens*. Is it so much to ask that we have faith that there is joy in our core? Is it really fitting for a 1 in 400 trillion miracle to wallow in low energy states?

As I've mentioned a few times, no one is expecting you to be a babbling brook of liquid rainbow happiness all the time. (In fact, some people might find it annoying if you were!) But no matter who you are, you are a unique and therefore special human being. And I have faith that you have joy available to you in your core, because we all do. It may take a little bit of effort and practise to learn to tap into it regularly. However, if you follow the recommendations in this book, make the choice to live in more joy and have absolute faith in your core joy, I am sure that you can change your life dramatically in ways you never imagined. And maybe even spew a few more joy rainbows now and then.

epilogue

Your Own Path To Joy

As much as I have tried to cover all my bases and give you a comprehensive 'toolbox', there is no cookie-cutter approach to bringing more joy into your life. You are a unique individual with your own needs, aptitudes and challenges. You may have tried meditation six different ways and just can't get into it. Don't sweat it! A morning gratitude practise might not work for you when the kids are jumping on your bed yelling for pancakes.

There are some basic components that I believe make up a joyful life: choice, a present-and-future focus, connection, gratitude, purpose, mindfulness, resilience and faith. And I have also pointed out some common archetypal paths to joy. Ultimately, however, you are going to have to forge your own path, something that works for *your* life.

Whether or not you realize it, you have already been forming a relationship with and a path to joy (even if you feel a little bit off the path). Hopefully, this book will serve as a landmark, a new starting point for your journey to deeper joy. And hopefully you have gained some clarity about what your new path might look like.

If you now feel that you know precisely what you are going to do and you are excited to hit the ground running and create a strong core of joy, that's great! Go for it! I know you will make tremendous strides, and I wish you well.

If you are still a little unsure about what all this might look like for you, that's fine, too. The wisdom of the Hermit card in the Tarot tells us that you don't have to know the whole path to take the first few steps. The lantern he carries only shines a few feet in front of him, but he can confidently walk from New York to Los Angeles in the dark with only the lantern. Just take a few first steps.

Start by making the initial choice to live with joy. Just make that choice *now*, and don't worry too much about the 'how'. Then, perhaps you can go back to the chapter on archetypal paths and write down a few activities, people or things that really bring you joy, and make a commitment to do, visit or see them a bit more often. Or, maybe decide on just *one* secondary choice that will support your decision: find a personal trainer to help you with an exercise routine, or make a weekly meal plan, or decide to count your blessings every night before you fall asleep.

Most of all, try to make it fun. After all, this is joy we're talking about here. I know I have said that there is some effort involved, but every worthwhile change is going to require a little bit of work. Yet at the same time, it needs to be fun too, or else, well, it kinda defeats the purpose, don't you think? We live in a high-pressure world, and many of us take even our happiness so goddamn seriously! I promise that if you are a high achiever, you are not going to slip and become a slacker by bringing more attention to joy. In fact, I would bet that you derive more meaning, satisfaction and even momentum from your achievements if they are framed in a context of joy.

I don't think I can say it enough: *you are a miraculous creature*. And I don't think it is too far-fetched to say that you can invite even more miraculous things into your life by focusing on your core joy. Approach it as a journey and don't worry too much about the destination. Make it unapologetically yours. Don't be too hard on yourself. I know you can do it, and deep down I think you do, too. Be authentically you and bring the joy!

references

'Chapter 01: Heart-Brain Communication.' *HeartMath Institute*, https://www.heartmath.org/research/science-of-the-heart/ heart-brain-communication/.

Allen, Summer. 'The Science of Gratitude: A white paper prepared for the John Templeton Foundation.' Greater Good Science Center, UC Berkeley, 2018, https://ggsc.berkeley.edu/ images/uploads/GGSC-JTF_White_Paper-Gratitude-FINAL.pdf

Brown, Brené. *The Gifts of Imperfection*. Random House, 2020.

Bustillos, Maria. 'How Cats Won the Internet.' *BBC Culture*, BBC, 21 Sept. 2015, https://www.bbc.com/culture/ article/20150918-how-did-cats-win-the-internet.

Byrne, Rhonda. *The Secret - The Magic*. Atria Books, 2012.

Csikszentmihalyi, Mihaly. *Flow: The psychology of optimal experience*. Harper & Row, 1990

Koenig, Harold G. 'Religion, Spirituality, and Health: The Research and Clinical Implications.' *ISRN Psychiatry*, U.S. National Library of Medicine, 16 Dec. 2012, https://www.ncbi. nlm.nih.gov/pmc/articles/PMC3671693/.

Krueger, Joachim. 'Flow and Happiness.' *Psychology Today*, Sussex Publishers, 26 Feb. 2015, https://www.psychologytoday. com/ca/blog/one-among-many/201502/flow-and-happiness.

Robbins, Tony. *Money: Master the Game*. Simon & Schuster Ltd, 2017.

Sincero, Jen. *You Are a Badass at Making Money: Master the Mindset of Wealth*. Penguin Books, an Imprint of Penguin Random House LLC, 2018.

www.ingramcontent.com/pod-product-compliance
Lightning Source LLC
LaVergne TN
LVHW050045090426
835510LV00043B/3024